The DELIGHTFUL HORROR
OF *Family Birding*

SHARING NATURE WITH THE NEXT GENERATION

The DELIGHTFUL HORROR OF *Family Birding*

SHARING NATURE WITH THE NEXT GENERATION

By Eli J. Knapp

Illustrations by John Rhett

TORREY HOUSE PRESS

SALT LAKE CITY • TORREY

First Torrey House Press Edition, October 2018
Copyright © 2018 by Eli J. Knapp

Published by Torrey House Press
Salt Lake City, Utah
www.torreyhouse.org

International Standard Book Number: 978-1-937226-91-6
E-book ISBN: 978-1-937226-92-3
Library of Congress Control Number: 2018932506

Illustrations by John Rhett
Cover design by Kathleen Metcalf
Interior design by Rachel Davis
Distributed to the trade by Consortium Book Sales and Distribution

Acknowledgements

Contents

INTRODUCTION

A touch of nature makes the whole world kin.

—William Shakespeare, *Troilus and Cressida*

The flat tire wasn't unexpected. We had already had half a dozen as we caravanned across the cheese-grater roads of East Africa. What I didn't expect, however, was a beautiful black-and-white bird with an outsized bill, just off the road from where our equally outsized truck had suddenly lurched to a stop. Toucan Sam leapt to mind. I had made a habit of identifying—and often failing to identify—the incredible wildlife with which Tanzania overflowed. Nearly every day of this semester abroad, I had thumbed through my ratty field guide and tried to focus my semi-functioning binoculars. This bird was new. It was some kind of hornbill. But what species? With at least twenty minutes to kill, I decided to find out. To do so, I needed a closer look.

I made my way past the twenty other students, somnolent in their seats, and climbed down out of the truck. Unsettled by the sudden bipedal commotion on this little-traveled dirt road, the ungainly bird flew deeper into the acacia scrub. Determined, I went in after it. I wove around several head-high thorn bushes and caught another sight of the bird. Just as I raised my binoculars, it flew off to another perch, deeper in. The bird and I followed this aggravating game of hide-and-seek for several minutes before it occurred to me that I should get back to the truck lest I hold up the gang.

I gave up on the bird and turned to head out the way I'd come. Just as before, I wove around thorn bushes. I expected to encounter the road . . . but no road appeared. I stopped and listened, hoping to catch sounds of my group. Nothing but the mechanical throb of cicadas. Despite the heat, a shiver ran down my spine, causing me to—against better judgment—pick up my pace. For several more minutes, I speed-walked through identical-looking trees, unwilling to admit a horrifying fact: I was lost. Not only was I lost, but I had no food, no water, and I seriously doubted whether anybody had seen me leave. Even worse, chances were that with the tire changed, they would unwittingly leave without me.

I willed myself to stop and regain composure. A breeze of hot, dry wind sent desiccated leaves swirling around my expensive, store-bought shoes. A black beetle scurried into a penny-sized hole in the hard-baked African soil. If only I could do the same. Here I was, a confident twenty-year-old, a recent member of the National Honor Society, yet more helpless than a newborn wildebeest.

Minutes dragged by, and the sun's rays increased their slant across the orange-red earth. I picked a direction, yelled a few times, and hoped for a response. None came. I glanced down at my watch. Surely the tire was changed by now. Ahead in the loose dirt, footprints! Hopeful, I bent down and examined them. My own. I was walking in circles.

In the midst of this new wave of panic, I heard the soft but unmistakable sound of bells. Bells! Was Santa's calendar skewed in Tanzania?! Savoring a rush of childlike giddiness, I beelined toward them. But it wasn't reindeer I found in the African bush; it was goats, dozens and dozens of them. Before I knew it, the amoeba-like herd engulfed me, munching on the move. I stood my ground as the unfazed animals marched around me, likely annoyed that I wasn't palatable. Where there were goats, I reasoned, there were people. And if there were people, I would be spared.

"People" turned out to be a knobby-kneed boy whose head maybe reached my belly button. A burgundy cloth hung from one shoulder and tied around his waist with a frayed piece of sisal. He couldn't have been older than twelve. Despite being startled to find a white guy out in the bush, he didn't run. He just stopped and looked at me, letting his goats disappear into the scrub.

Since my Swahili wasn't good enough to explain my predicament, I dropped to one knee and sketched a line in the dirt with a small stick. Then I tried to imitate a truck's diesel engine. Wordlessly, the boy watched my poor charade, nodding slightly. Then, he spun on his heels and started walking. His herd—all his responsibility—was abandoned.

I followed like an imprinted duckling. There was no way this boy was going to get away, even if it meant ending up in a distant village. Fifteen minutes later, we popped out on a road—my road. Fifty yards away was the truck. The driver was tightening lug nuts with a large tire iron, and the other students, oblivious to my panic-stricken absence, were playing hacky sack in the road. I hadn't been missed at all.

Overcome with relief, I pantomimed for the boy to stay, that I wanted to give him something. I ran to the truck, rummaged through my duffel bag, and found some Matchbox cars I had brought to Africa as token gifts. Perfect. I grabbed them, jumped off the truck, and ran back. The boy was gone.

Immanuel Kant once wrote, "Man is the only being who needs education." What Kant didn't clarify, however, was what form of education man needs. As I discovered in the Tanzanian bush, my fifteen years of western-based education held little practicality.

For life skills, I had nothing on the young goatherd.

Knowledge comes in many ways and from many sources. Most of mine up to that point had come in the controlled environment of a classroom. My teachers held forth in typical classrooms, in which teachers teach and students learn. In Tanzania, my education was upended. It became experiential, and much of it came from nature itself. And my learning, I quickly realized, came from unexpected sources, including small goatherds.

These lessons were hardly profound. Now, as a parent and a college professor, it seems I relearn them weekly. The essays in this book chronicle this journey. At times, it's been difficult and disorienting. But it's been delightful, too.

Life has afforded me new eyes to see nature. In that rollercoaster year before we wed, Linda called me excitedly from work in Santa Barbara.

"Is everything okay?" I asked, unused to her calling midday.

"There's a beautiful yellow-orange bird outside my window! It has a black bib," she added.

"Is it a goldfinch or a house finch?" I asked, naming the first birds to come to mind.

"The bill is too slender," she replied confidently. Not yet keen to the west coast birds, I couldn't come up with an alternative.

"Can you draw it?" I asked. She came from a family of artists—I was confident she could.

"I'll try."

Later that night, Linda produced a sketch she'd done on a piece of scrap paper. Just a few simple but well-placed lines. Quick, yes. But obvious field marks and expert proportions. No doubt a hooded oriole. I was smitten, both with the bird and the artist. This was—and is—who she is. Linda overflows with curiosity about the natural world. While I'm obsessed with the creatures around us, Linda's more balanced, thank heavens. While she'll crane her neck out a window to see a cool bird, I'll career down a ravine. Our mutual interest is expressed differently but unites us nonetheless. I held onto the sketch for years. Fortunately, I've held onto Linda even longer. Her influence on my journey and that of our children lies behind the stories that follow.

I used to think I'd wait to write a nature book until my kids had grown up and left. But then I entered the forest with Linda, my kids, and later my college students. Everything changed. With Ezra, Indigo, and Willow at my side, I saw nature through young, impressionable lenses. Wonder deepened; the same wonder I'd felt watching the hornbill in the featureless thorn scrub. The richest book I could create, I realized, would be one that captures this wonder in the mixed-up, rarely planned moments that make up life.

I am an odd duck: a hybrid anthropologist-ecologist by trade who happens to have a special love of birds and nature. While I haven't forced these interests on my kids, I have immersed them in it. A feeder is visible from every window of our house, and bird paraphernalia—carvings, feathers, and field guides—line every shelf. I even named one daughter Indigo after one of my favorite birds, the indigo bunting (I may or may not have known that another group of birds, the indigobirds, are renowned for their ability to parasitize other birds). A second daughter, Willow, is bird-friendly nomenclature as well. More than occasionally, however, I overdo it.

"No more birds, Dad!" Ezra occasionally shouts from the back seat after I've pulled over to get a better look at an overflying raptor. But in between his back seat directives, I've caught him craning his neck, too.

A few years ago, while enjoying a family dinner around the

table, Ezra, then six years old, couldn't conceal his mushrooming bird knowledge. "We're going to go around in a circle and everybody is going to tell us what their day's highlight was," I had instructed, attempting to rein in the raucous dinner cacophony, focus the kids' attention on mealtime, and teach them to take turns speaking.

"I'll go first," Ezra said, waving a macaroni noodle around on his fork like a baton. "I saw an indigo bunting while on the bus today! It was by the big bend in the road," he added, as if more detail would verify his claim. His blue eyes held mine, waiting for my reaction. While he loved to get a rise out of me, this time at least, he wasn't ruffling my feathers.

I have no idea if any of my kids—or my students—will one day enjoy nature as much as I do. But at the very least, they'll be familiar with it. Since enjoyment is contingent upon understanding, familiarity seems like a step in the right direction.

This collection of essays spans a five-year period of my life as a fledgling father. They're arranged thematically, not sequentially. As a result, the ages of my children fluctuate forward and backward, which may be disconcerting to the careful reader. Rest assured, I haven't sired any Benjamin Buttons. While ages change, the mutual learning we all undergo doesn't. Nor does our discovery of knowledge in unexpected places, or our collective familial decision to let nature lead.

One of the unexpected places popping up often in these pages is Africa. The continent has shaped my family mightily over the years, luring us back in spite of our best attempts to put down deeper roots in the States. Africa first called us as students and now as professors. Linda and I teach, yes. But we still learn far more, annually treated to profound lessons from wise and generous people that live far closer to the land than we do.

All the stories emerge from my experiences as a husband, father, professor, and lifelong lover of birds and nature. Some of these experiences have been delightful, some horrible, and most a combination thereof. This book, like life, isn't about a destination. Rather, it's about process, false starts, and learning from mistakes. It's a book that shows that the youngest among us may appreciate nature best, and that life is at its richest when we go outdoors together and keep our eyes open. Lastly, it's a book about coddiwompling. Like the ivory-billed woodpecker, this word doesn't seem to exist regardless of how badly I want it to. Its definition: traveling in a purposeful manner toward a vague destination. This book examines the intersection of our lives with birds. Hopefully it begets a relationship. Where that relationship ends up is anybody's guess. Perhaps to greater knowledge, deeper introspection, or a more satisfying view of nature. A little ambiguity is good; I'm convinced that the best paths take us to places we didn't know we wanted to go.

Dr. Elliott Coues, a wild-eyed birder from a former century who did his share of coddiwompling, once wrote: "For myself, the time is past, happily or not, when every bird was an agreeable surprise, for dewdrops do not last all day; but I have never walked in the woods without learning something that I did not know before . . . how can you, with so much before you, keep out of the woods another minute?"

Like Coues, I can't keep out of the woods another minute. So I may as well take my kids, my students, everyone. Nature has so much to teach us. To learn, we may have to give up control and let nature lead. Maybe, like the birds, we all just need to wing it.

Part 1

THROUGH A CHILD'S EYES

Stellar's jay

1 · THE ONLY THINGS TO FEAR

Ah! Reader, could you but know the emotion that then agitated my breast.

—John James Audubon

"Kestrels! They're attacking!" my brother, Andrew, yelled from his sleeping bag. Three birds had landed on the railing above him, shattering the pre-dawn silence with cacophonous calls.

Andrew and I had spent the night sleeping out on the small deck of my red ramshackle cabin. Now he was determined to get back inside. Unwilling to shed the pseudo-shield his sleeping bag provided, however, Andrew chose to roll over me in my own sleeping bag, crawl to the door, and lurch inside like a clumsy, overgrown caterpillar. As the door slammed, I heard him collapse on the floor.

I lay still on the deck, watching the birds as a mischievous Grinchian smile spread across my face. The alleged kestrels were not kestrels at all. They were Steller's jays. This particular trio had been visiting my cabin's deck for several months now. As an outdoor educator in Central California, I'd been granted a closet-sized cabin with a slightly more spacious deck, just big enough for two sleeping bags to lie parallel. Impossibly tall redwood trees amid a carpet of ferns lent a fairytale feel to the forest enveloping the cabin. In my mind, it was a perfect setting for a band of clever, cobalt-colored birds.

But not in Andrew's mind. It was just after six a.m. The jays had come down with their typical homicidal cries, proclaiming their right to the meager peanut offering I always put out the night before. To Andrew who lacked prior exposure, it appeared an outright avian assault: dark-crested villains swooping down through the gloaming, hell-bent on snatching souls. Since he'd arrived only the day before, I had forgotten to mention the routine, early morning visit of the obstreperous jays. Together, we'd decided to sleep out on the deck. Serendipitously, he chose a position right by the railing. It was too good a prank to be premeditated. Stellar indeed.

My delight then, as now, spawns from the competitive nature my brothers and I share. Our competitiveness is so intense it spills over into sibling schadenfreude, or pleasure derived from the misfortune of others. Despite being four years younger, Andrew is far more academically gifted. He processes information faster, his memory is better, and in most areas where I struggle, he excels effortlessly. So whenever I discover a chink in his impressive armor, I exploit it. The misidentification of a bird accompanied by a hysterical, panic-stricken reaction was a gaping chink, the height of schadenfreude. As the last jay lifted off my railing and the avian apocalypse ended, I knew I had sweet fodder to turn him red-faced for years.

I gained something else from my brother's misfortune: insight. Though the incident seemed trivial at the time, I learned that Andrew had fears I lacked. I spent the bulk of my youth in the woods. Andrew didn't; he was an indoors kid. To me, birds were familiar, and I sought them out. Not so, for him. He co-existed with them. To him, birds were backdrop, noticed only when they hit the windshield or woke him up.

Andrew wasn't culpable for his indifference; we merely differed in our formative influences. Nature-oriented friends and teachers dragged me into the fields and forests throughout my childhood. Obviously, kestrels don't attack sleeping men in redwood forests. But Andrew's lack of experience, punctuated by an unexpected blitzkrieg of birds, translated into misapprehension and fear.

Now, as a professor, I routinely hear echoes of my brother's experience in the lives of students enrolled in my ornithology course. Often hesitantly, and without much eye contact, a student admits to having a fear of birds. The first few times this happened, I had to force a deadpan response. Cheerful robins and beautiful bluebirds leapt to mind. How could anyone be scared of these colorful feathered friends that fill the air with joyous melody? "Can you elaborate?" I'd ask, clenching my jaw to prevent a smile. Most of their explanations were vague and ambiguous. But finally, this past spring, I confirmed the suspicion I had gained way back in the redwood forest.

"I'm here because I need to get some science credits and . . ." Emily said, her voice trailing off.

"And what?" I asked, curious.

"Well, because . . . I'm scared of birds." She stared at her desk as her face turned the color of a cardinal. Here we go again, I thought, gripping my podium to squelch any potential sarcastic reply. The class giggled, and several students smirked at one another.

"So I'm here to get over my fear," Emily finished. This wasn't the time for a cross-examination. She had been brave, and I wasn't going to add any further public humiliation. I moved on to the next student but made a mental note to follow up with her if an opportunity presented itself later on in the course.

"The only thing we have to fear is fear itself," Franklin Delano Roosevelt memorably proclaimed back in 1933. Catchy as his words were, Roosevelt could have used a fact-checker. In 1960, for example, researchers Gibson and Walk discovered that humans innately fear falling. Several decades later, another researcher, William Falls, determined that even as babies, we startle at loud noises. Culture has nothing to do with these innate fears, and they're exceedingly difficult to undo. We learn all our other fears along life's path, picking them up like odd-shaped pebbles. While lots of people fear snakes, we're not born that way; we acquire it from our culture and our environment, taking most of our cues from our parents. My wife, Linda, for example, grew up in West Africa. There, many snakes were venomous. She was taught that the only good snake was a dead snake. The opposite was true for me in the friendly snake world of the northeastern United States.

An inveterate collector of flora and fauna, I have shown my son, Ezra, dozens of snakes and bugs ever since his diaper days. And when Linda wasn't looking, I gave him many to play with. So it came as no surprise one day to find him chasing Linda through the yard as she yelled at him to stop. Confusion was on his face then, while a little green snake dangled from his hands. Why was his mother scared, if his father wasn't? Even more unsurprisingly, and to Linda's great consternation, Ezra's early confusion soon morphed into devilishness as that initial chase evolved into an episodic—and highly cherished—game. Needless to say, I bring home far fewer snakes than I used to. Not that I need to. Now he collects them himself.

While fear can be learned, it can also be paralyzing. In the 1920s, Walter Bradford Cannon coined "fight or flight" to describe key behaviors that may occur in the context of perceived threat. Although oversimplified, I like the way neuroscientist Seth Norrholm described it. Fear, he wrote, can cause us to take the "low road or the high road." If the brain's sensory system detects something to fear, adrenaline kicks in, our hearts beat faster, and we get the classic fight or flight response. Once we journey down this low road, our fight or flight may malfunction, causing us to freeze like the proverbial deer in the headlights.

Recent research suggests, however, that freezing may be adaptive too, not a malfunction at all. When fleeing or aggressive responses are likely to be ineffective, freezing may be the best option. Like possums that play dead, we freezers experience "tonic immobility," which "includes motor and vocal inhibition with an abrupt initiation and cessation." Judging from the number of times I've turned to stone as my two-year-old daughter momentarily chokes on a piece of food, I'm a bona fide freezer. Even though it may be an adaptive response for the possum, it hasn't seemed so for me, especially as a father with young kids. In the language of Norrholm, I've lived on the low road.

If my wife hears our little girl even faintly sputter, however, she will grab the baby, pat her back, and save the day with nary a quickened pulse. My wife may be afraid of snakes. But with choking and innumerable other injuries and accidents, she takes the high road every time. We take the high road, Norrholm suggests, when our sensory system signals a higher cortical center in the brain. I've seen this before, our brain thinks, so there's no reason to panic. Studies show that through repeated exposure, we can overcome our fears and act more reasonably, even in frightening situations.

A problem, of course, is that new things—things we can't prepare for—happen to us all the time. This past summer, for example, nine-year-old Ezra and I went for a jog on an old railroad bed in Big Pocono State Park, in Pennsylvania. A quarter mile into our journey, we met up with a panic-stricken man and his wife. "We just saw a bear!" the man said, glancing over his shoulder as if the bruin were stalking him.

"It was big!" His wife spread her arms wide.

"How long ago?" I asked.

"Just now." The man glanced at his watch as if to verify his claim. "It crossed the path and went down a hill. You can keep going if you want to," he added, "but we're getting out of here!" With that, the couple power walked on down the trail.

I was torn. The couple's fear was palpable. Unsurprisingly, culture had saturated me with a fear of bears that borders on paranoia. At the same time, I'd encountered bears before and knew that, while attacks do happen, they're exceedingly rare. If we kept going down the trail, yes, I was taking a risk. But if I turned tail and fled, I would be sending a message to my son. It would tell him that woods with bears were scary woods. Since bears have repopulated so many rural areas, this could put him on edge the rest of his life. I know many people who are too scared to enter the woods. Nature—the dark and scary forest—so rarely gets a fair shake in fairy tales and children's books. I didn't want to perpetuate such misplaced fear in real life.

But I knew that fear, whether innate or learned, is a good adaptive behavior. Without it, the human race likely wouldn't exist, as it helped us survive predators and identify threats in the landscape. Had the infamous dodo bird on Mauritius been more timorous, the hospitable species might have been able to avoid the avarice of the Dutch sailors who, legend has it, clubbed the amiable birds with the same cooking pots they tossed them into. Through no fault of its own, the dodo never learned to fear bipedal brutes with wide eyes and empty stomachs.

American culture, in contrast, overplays the unusual. As a result, we've been brainwashed to fear many things in nature and all things ursine. A car accident rarely merits a news story. A bear attack, which stirs the imagination of our inner Neanderthal, demands the front page. I have a friend who, right or wrong, once grabbed his four-year-old daughter and ran upon hearing rustling noises in a blackberry patch. Today, his daughter wants nothing to do with trails and hiking. Yes, it could have been a bear. But I've also heard many "bears" myself that turned out to be one-and-a-half-ounce eastern towhees foraging in the leaf litter.

"What do you say, Ez?" I asked, looking down at him. "Should we keep going?"

"Let's do it!" he said without hesitating. As he had with the snakes I'd given him years earlier, he lived on the high road.

"Okay, but be ready to shoot up a tree if I say so!" I instructed. Slowly, we continued down the railroad bed. Sure enough, two hundred yards later, we spied a large black bear sunning on a fallen log quite a distance down the hill. It was a magnificent sight, the bear utterly at peace in its leafy green world. For a while, we watched side by side, saying little. Seeing a bear from the confines of a moving car is one thing. On foot, however, there are whispers of instruction, buzzing insects, and heightened senses of being alive. Like lifting all the cages at a zoo. Sharing the moment made it that much better.

Since leaving the sun-seeking bear in the Pocono Mountains, I've hesitated to relay the details of our bear encounter—the decision to advance or retreat—to others. I've grown leery of culture-influenced, risk-averse mindsets. I've thought it through quite a bit, however. Yes, there were risks. But risks, I've realized, are greatly influenced by perception. We may not perceive the risk of riding in a car because we do it so much, but it's still far riskier than walking in the woods. Everything I do with my son carries risk: taking him to the playground, teaching him to ride a bike, jumping on a trampoline. Even bringing him into the world was a risk. If you focus on all the things that can go wrong in these normal, everyday activities, it's pretty scary. The flipside, however—incapacitating fear—is far scarier. In the context of healthy, long-term development and self-confidence, what's the best road to take?

An opportune time finally came during ornithology class. We

had gone on several field trips and studied lots of different birds. Emily had birded like all the others, and the fear she expressed on the first day had hardly seemed paralyzing. On the way home from a local wetland, Emily was sitting shotgun. "So, Emily," I asked as nonchalantly as I could, "why are you scared of birds?"

"I'm not really sure," she answered, looking out her window.

"Did you have a bad experience? Was it too many Hitchcock movies?"

Silence. Emily's hesitation made me fear (a learned fear, of course) I'd overstepped.

After a long pause, she said, "I can't remember, but I'm sure it was irrational. All I know is that it started when I was little." She again fell silent, then turned to me with a wry smile. "By the way, I'm not scared of birds anymore."

I hoped it was true. Emily's lack of exposure to the animal world, like my brother's, was no fault of her own. Unfamiliarity had relegated her to the low road. But Emily was no dodo. Within a few weeks of going out in the field, she'd intentionally gotten to know some of the creatures she shares a planet with. Even better, she learned to call most of them by name. To get there, all she'd needed—all any of us need, really—is a decision to take the high road.

A murder of crows

2 · ONE SHORT OF A PARLIAMENT

There was an old man who told me when I was a boy that I should look at words like beautiful stones. He said I should lift each one and look at it from all sides before I used it. Then I would respect it.

—Kent Nerbern, *Neither Wolf Nor Dog*

"That's the third murder we've witnessed today!" I remark to seven-year-old Ezra, sitting in the front seat of the tandem kayak we're paddling.

"What?" Ezra asks. "What do you mean?" Of all the characteristics of kids, unbridled curiosity may be my favorite. I prey upon it. And now, I was doing exactly that.

"You mean you didn't see that murder?" Water droplets drip from my paddle and roll down my forearm. "Well, surely you had to hear it? Listen! You can still hear it!" Ezra swivels in his seat and catches my smirk.

"You mean, the crows?" he asks quizzically.

"Yeah. Did you know that a group of crows is called a 'murder'?"

"No." Ezra swivels back in his seat and resumes paddling in a rare moment of thoughtful silence. He's somewhat rankled. Like most seven-year-olds, he'd rather be teaching me than vice-versa. But his curiosity trumps all. I know what's coming, and Ezra doesn't let me down.

"Why?"

Despite my anticipation of the question, I have absolutely

no idea. Much like a crow, I'm an inveterate scavenger. Only, I prefer to pick from the carcass of oddball natural history trivia. On one such foray, I'd stumbled upon the collective noun. Collective nouns are those that describe groupings of individuals. For people, like "crew" or "party," they're kind of boring. For birds and animals, they're anything but. How had I lived much of my life, I'd wondered on my day of discovery, without the nutrients of these nuggets? Like other collectors, I'd quickly amassed a precious horde. In my merriment, I neglected the more laborious work of figuring out why these monikers stuck.

My son had exposed my ignorance. Now I'm the rankled one. Like most proud fathers, I can't let him know that. So I play the ignoble card and deftly redirect the conversation.

"Isn't 'murder' such a cooler word than 'flock'?" I remark. "And the word for a group of ravens is even cooler. It's an 'unkindness'!"

"Why?" Ezra asks again. I try one last time to dodge.

"But some group names are dumb. Do you see those killdeer on the rocks?" I point with my paddle.

"Yeah."

"Well, a group of plovers like them is called a 'congregation.'"

"Why don't you like that word, Dad?"

"Because it's too hard to say. Too many syllables."

"I don't think it's hard to say." Ezra pronounces "congregation" aloud. He has a knack for exposing my double standards and duplicities.

"Yeah, I guess not. I just don't like it."

The cawing of the crows is replaced by the gentle sounds of our paddles in the calm water. We both fall silent, our thoughts expanding like the ripples from our bow. While Ezra likely dwells on the underwater whirlpools he creates with his paddle, I dredge the dumpster of the other collective nouns I'd stuck in my mental scrapbook.

The ones I liked best were the ones that seemed so apt; so descriptive of their species. Jays, for example, are strident birds. When their dander is up, they can awaken a sleeping forest, or a sleeping man in a forest, in milliseconds. The Steller's jay, as my brother discovered in the redwoods of California, is the worst offender. So the collective noun—a "scold" of jays—is apropos. The same logic applies for several other species. Anybody who has watched hundreds of starlings suddenly descend upon a lawn in fall and the monotone cacophony that results will agree that a "murmuration" of starlings is ideal. As for ravens, an "unkindness" suits their dark and brooding demeanor. More lighthearted is the name for a group of ring-necked pheasants. Although it's only happened once, I'll never forget the sea of colors when a family of pheasants exploded from a hedgerow in front of me. It was indeed a "bouquet" of pheasants, a term that must have arisen from an artistically minded naturalist. Or perhaps a love-struck hunter on his way home to his damsel.

Other collective nouns are special for the sheer winsome joy they create. Sure, a flock of goldfinches is fine. But goldfinches, especially when they adorn my coneflowers like Christmas ornaments in late summer, deserve more than that. So yes, I call them a "charm." The same goes for larks. When meadowlarks alight from a flowery field, they are far more than a flock. They truly are an "exultation" of larks. And when I someday see a group of eagles soaring in the sky, I'm sure I'll agree that they're a "convocation" indeed.

I've collected other collective nouns too. But these I'd like to purge. They clutter my mind like mental tchotchkes. Like a "congregation" of plovers (which should be a "panic," mind you), these nouns remain on the shelves of my mind, gathering dust. Some simply need to be reversed. Everybody knows that a "descent" of woodpeckers should actually be an ascent, for woodpeckers only go up tree trunks, not down. Descent, while rich and descriptive, should be reserved for the devil down-heads—the nuthatches.

Some need to be jettisoned altogether. Bobolinks live in open fields. They migrate thousands of miles between the Americas, and their otherworldly song is unfettered and free. A "chain" of bobolinks doesn't fit. Chains and imperialism should be reserved for the house sparrows that have usurped lands from many natives. And while I'm at it, how about a "siege" of herons? Get serious. Most herons are downright stoics, far more content to watch than lay siege. Yes, they suddenly launch forward like lightning when an unsuspecting fish swims by. But this is no siege. Wouldn't a "seize" of herons suit them better?

As soon as I return the kayak to its perch in the garage and the last droplet has evaporated from my paddle, I set to researching how the odd collective nouns came to be. The first thing I realize is that they're old: from 1486, to be precise. The Dame Juliana Barnes was tossing them about in the Book of St. Albans before Columbus even thought of sailing the ocean blue. Wow.

Less surprising is the fact that many of the terms were associated with the three important H's of the day: hunting, heraldry, and hawking. Since European culture had a monopoly on these pursuits and flowery written expression, credit is typically accorded therein. My hunch tells me that Native Americans devised collective nouns far earlier. How could the Blackfeet people not have used their own unique terms when a few hundred thousand bison rumbled by? Something akin to a rumble? A thunder? Maybe more aptly, a buffet? How did millions of salmon linguistically inspire the Chinook? And billions of passenger pigeons the Shawnee people?

But we're stuck with recorded history. And a bouquet of

pheasants probably seemed all the more fragrant when a well-trained hawk was bringing one back for the dinner table. The other colorful collectives got their foothold in mythology and folklore. Owls, for example, were the symbol for the Greek goddess of wisdom, Athena. Due to their learned disposition, a group of them resembled a "parliament." Crows, on the other hand, evidently held trials to mete out punishments for their fellow corvid transgressors. Those found guilty were executed by the flock. In his book *Mind of the Raven*, noted ecologist Bernd Heinrich adds credence to the myth with actual observation of such events. "This killing was a severe punishment," Heinrich writes, describing a raven homicide in his aviary. "It went far beyond the usual behavior aimed at repelling a competitor from a cache or for showing displeasure over a mild infraction. This was censure of the severest kind." In my wooded corner of the Northeast, some mornings I'm awakened when the corvid cacophony reaches fever pitch. On such mornings, I pull the pillow over my head and thank the Lord I'm not a transgressing crow.

I may not have transgressed as a crow, but I nearly have as a professor. My most recent near-transgression occurred after I dragged a gaggle of students out for an evening of owling. We had spent the day straining our necks trying to make sense of the "confusion" of warblers (another appropriate collective noun). With the course set to end in a week, I wanted to leave the students with an experience they'd never forget. One they'd tell their friends about. And one that ultimately would keep a flame of outdoor appreciation burning forever. Among all the birds, owls do this best. So I'd brought the students out to a nameless swamp to find my most reliable owl, a barred owl that had never failed to regale my student squadrons. He had benevolently revealed himself for five straight years.

Not this year. We had entered the woods edging the swamp

silently and were now reclining on the forest floor. The students were quiet, the sky was dark, and the trees were still. It was a perfect night for an owl. But my owl apparently didn't think so. Silence except for the greedy hum of the mosquito swarms. We sat. Twenty minutes elapsed. Thirty. The woods grew so dark I could hardly make out the forms of my students. And knowing their discouragement, I was glad I couldn't.

Finally, I got up to leave, and the students followed suit. On a lark (an exaltation!), I tried one last owl imitation, beseeching the avian gods to send down an ambassador.

Miraculously, the gods acquiesced. On silent wings, a barred owl barreled across the sky and landed just above on a broken branch sticking perpendicularly out of a gnarled white pine. He looked down at us, swiveled his head in the mechanical way that owls do, and then rent the silence with the best who-cooks-for-you rendition I'd ever heard. Despite my earlier admonitions for silence, several students audibly gasped. And then, to top it off, a second owl flew in and called. This excited the first owl, which took up where the second let off. Silhouetted, the two owls worked themselves into a dither. In the midst of their performance, I motioned for the students to follow me out of the forest. My owl had delivered yet again. The rest of the night belonged to him and his consort.

Back in the van, the students broke loose with stories of awe and astonishment. I listened attentively, my grin spreading ear to ear. I was relieved. But also joyful. Here was the transformative power of encountering a special creature on its own terms. Even in our cyber world where experiences are increasingly virtualized, these desensitizing layers of abstraction can peel away with one barred owl. Or two, in our case.

One of my former students, Laura, had caught wind of our evening trip and stashed herself in the van for another visit with the owl. Having had me as a professor before, she'd grown accustomed to my love of the collective noun. Amidst the owl outpouring, Laura called out from the back, "Eli, we were just one short of a parliament!"

"Aren't two owls enough for a parliament?" I shot back. While I agreed with her, I couldn't resist a chance to play the role of devil's advocate. Laura smiled but didn't respond. She had no answer.

Neither did I. And I still don't. According to most dictionaries, a group is two or more individuals. Since a "parliament" refers to a group, technically two should suffice. But a parliament, at least the parliament my mind conjures up of bombastic British folk in wigs, definitely needs a roomful. I'm with Laura. As mesmerizing as the owls were, we saw a pair, not a parliament.

Several months later I got a package in the mail with Laura's return address on it. I opened it up and pulled out a young-adult book with a forgettable picture on the front. The pathetic title had me smiling nonetheless. *Owl's Well That Ends Well.* Indeed, owl was well. While we may have missed a parliament during our night of owling, I had learned yet again that the only predictable part of nature is its unpredictability.

This attribute—while at times excruciating—is what I relish most. It's why I'll keep luring my son along on kayaking trips and marching students into swamps. Because even if I end up one short of a parliament, I may yet be given a charm or bouquet. And if I hear a scold or a murmuration emanating out of the darkest part of the woods, I'll be extra alert. Because I never know when I'll witness another murder.

Hooded merganser

3 · NOTHING TO SNEEZE AT

I enter a swamp as a sacred place, a sanctum sanctorum.

—Henry David Thoreau

"But Daaaad, I wanna go birding, too!"

"Ezra, wouldn't you rather stay home and play with your Legos?"

"No. I wanna go birding!"

I was poised by the door, binoculars and camera in my bag, ready for a brief blitz on a nearby swamp to see hooded mergansers that only show up in my corner of New York in the fall, on migration. This was my only chance to see them. But here was my four-year-old son begging to come along. I looked hard at my skinny, blond-haired boy, who was imploring me like a prosecutor whose life depended on this one case.

"Do you really want to come?"

"Yeah, I wanna be with you," Ezra replied in the sincere tone known only to small children. Ouch. My guilty conscience grew heavier by the second. If I went alone, I'd have the chance of seeing mergansers. If Ez tagged along, I'd exchange the shy mergansers for father/son time. With Ezra's larynx on board, we'd be lucky to see a mallard. It is the ultimate dilemma of young parents who love birding and other outdoor pursuits that require patience, stealth, and quiet. Perhaps there was still a way out.

"Why don't you check with Mom?" I hoped to high heaven

Linda had other plans for him, like a bath perhaps. Ezra disappeared into the living room. He returned instantly.

"Mom said I can go." He clapped his hands. "And I've already got my shoes on!"

My heart sank. While I love time with my kids, I also cherish solitude.

"Okay, Ez, but when we get to the pond, you have to promise not to make a sound. We're going to see some really shy birds." I knew we wouldn't see the birds, but I still had to try.

"I promise, Dada."

We had a great drive to the lake, chatting about all things from Hot Wheels to telephone poles. But upon arrival at the well-wooded lake, I admonished Ezra again about the need for quiet. Solemnly, he nodded understanding.

I scanned the waters and saw a flock of likely mergansers at the far edge. We'd have to approach stealthily through the woods.

"Ready, Ez?"

"I'm ready, Dada."

"Okay, let's go. Remember, don't make a sound." We entered a thick stand of conifers and slowly picked our way to the other side of the lake, being careful not to step on loud twigs and leaves. Ezra mimicked every footstep I took and never said a word. "We're almost there," I whispered. "Great job." Ezra smiled back and flashed me a thumbs-up.

We crouched low behind a log and slowly lifted our heads. There they were. Right in front of us, two doting male mergansers paddled alongside half a dozen earth-toned females. The afternoon sun's slanting rays lit up the males' white head crests like flags of surrender. Wanting to remember the scene, I pulled out my camera and snapped a few shots. Euphoric, I glanced at Ezra to see if he was enjoying it, too.

He wasn't. His smile was gone. His eyes were pinched shut, his cheeks were red, and he had both hands covering his mouth. Uh-oh.

"Ez, are you okay?" He nodded his head feebly but wouldn't open his eyes or pull his hands away from his mouth. Confused, I picked him up and crashed back out through the woods, this time oblivious to the sound we made. When we reached the roadside, I set him down.

"AAAAHHHH-CHOO!" Ezra's head shot forward like a released bowstring. He hacked, sputtered and wheezed. As for me, I started laughing uncontrollably. In between laughter, I turned to Ezra.

"Why did you wait so long to sneeze?!"

"You said not to make a sound!"

"Well done, Ez! Did you see those beautiful mergansers?"

"What mergansers?" he replied matter-of-factly. I doubled over again.

The setting October sun lit up the orange-red trees like flames as we drove home. With his colossal sneeze now behind him, Ezra made up for lost time, filling the air with a string of questions and non sequitur proclamations typical of a four year old. It's a time I'll treasure someday when he's an uncommunicative and self-conscious teenager.

The decision to bird or spend time with Ezra needn't be an either/or. I've learned it's a both/and. We had time together, made a priceless memory, and I even saw my birds.

Next time maybe Ezra will see them, too.

Northern flicker

4 · A Flicker of Life

There is special providence in the fall of a sparrow.

—William Shakespeare, *Hamlet*

"Eli, you have to *do* something! Oh, I can't bear to watch this!" I leapt out of my chair in the other room and rushed to the sound of my wife's voice. Few words could prompt such immediate action. But these words I feared.

As I rounded the corner into the living room, my adrenalized fear suddenly ebbed. Everybody was alive. Linda, six-year-old Ezra, and three-year-old Indigo stood shoulder-to-shoulder at the window, eyes downcast. They appeared to be—and were—attending a wake.

There on the deck lay a northern flicker. Seen from afar, these ant-obsessed birds are arresting, an intricate hodge-podge of speckles and stripes. Up close, they are downright exquisite—as if a zebra and leopard lent their patterns to a professional painter. This was a male, his black moustache (or "malar stripe") slicing down his cheeks.

The silence was a rare counterpoint to our typical household cacophony. And it matched the flicker's motionless body. Until it convulsed, flipping its head back over its body as its yellow-splashed wings whipped outward. And then it convulsed again. And again.

Linda, ever empathetic to anything with a pulse (with a glaring—and hypocritical—exception of mice and snakes), couldn't help herself. "I can't take this!" Her voice faltered as she sped out of the room. Ezra, unable to endure his mother's despair, ran after her, mimicking her saddening shrieks. That left Indigo and I alone at the funeral.

Although I had already pieced together the puzzle due to the new smudges on the window's exterior, I couldn't resist quizzing my uncharacteristically stoical three-year-old.

"What happened?" I asked, looking down at her.

"The birdie hit the window," she said, without any trace of emotion. "Is it dead?" I said nothing as the flicker flipped one last time and then lay lifeless. My daughter's question hung in the air like the birdfeeder hanging five feet above the flicker's head. Wishing again for parental blueprints of when to introduce what, I decided this was a moment of truth.

"Yeah, it's dead," I replied.

As soon as I said this, one of my western New York heroes, Roger Tory Peterson, came to mind. It was simple association. Growing up in nearby Jamestown, New York, he was captivated by this very species, the northern flicker, as an eleven-year-old boy. Similarly, he had discovered a listless flicker on an oak branch near his home. Not knowing if it was dead or asleep, Peterson picked it up and cradled it. The next moment, the flicker sprang back to life and exploded from his arms. The bird had only been temporarily impaired or perhaps exhausted after a long migration.

This phenomenon of sudden recoveries is not uncommon to homeowners who feed birds and witness window collisions that temporarily render birds witless. What surprised me was that this was a flicker, a woodpecker that smashes its head against immovable objects for a living. Woodpeckers are equipped with the very best concussion prevention gear available. Micro-CT scans have revealed tiny pockets of air—shock absorbers—in the woodpecker's skull, unlike the solid-wall skulls of most other birds. Another small cushion sits between the base of the bill and the skull. The most effective of the flicker's evolutionary airbags, however, may be the remarkable tongue. Unlike all other birds, woodpecker tongues connect to the hyoid bone, which exits the skull at the base and wraps up and over the skull, anchoring to the forehead. The wraparound tongue isn't just a cushion; it's also a tourniquet. It effectively pinches the jugular vein while the bird hammers away, increasing the volume of blood within the skull. This softens the impact within the skull rather than just outside it.

These adaptations explain why affiliates from the concussion-prone NFL have shown a sudden interest in bird watching. They may also account for the recovery of young Peterson's flicker. Regardless, he found the moment miraculous. So miraculous, in fact, that he credited it with changing the course of his life and leading him into a life of birds. This soon spawned his famous field guides. And it was my father's Peterson guide to the birds of eastern North America, which I flipped through incessantly as a boy by the windowsill, which helped lead me into a life of bird appreciation. So I owe a debt to the flicker as well.

But Peterson's flicker had resurrected. This one, with rumpled feathers and clouded eyes, needed interment. So out the door I walked. Untouched by the empathetic spillover shown by her mother and brother, Indigo followed me out the door. I bent over the flicker and picked it up. Without any prompting, Indigo extended her index finger and slid it delicately along the bird's back. I studied her face as she did so. Her slightly furrowed brow and focused gaze revealed little. Then, as the tip of her small forefinger disappeared in the fullness of the flicker's feathers, her eyebrows went up, almost imperceptibly. When her finger reemerged toward the tail feathers, she smiled and her entire demeanor softened with wonder. Wordlessly, I mimicked her motion. Together, our two forefingers working as one, we smoothed out the bird's rumpled back. Dignity had now been added to this death.

Having ironed out the bird's burial cloak, Indigo looked up at me. "Are you going to bury it, Daddy?"

"Yes," I replied.

"Good," she said, apparently satisfied with this proper course of action.

I cradled the bird with two hands, stepped down off the deck, and went around to the back of the house. I couldn't resist stealing a glance back at my daughter. She remained rooted, statuesque, watching me. Her stillness, so rare in her busybody stage of life, spoke volumes. This was a small and sacred moment. While its meaning was unclear, I knew only that it mattered.

I grabbed a shovel from the garage, dug a hole, and gently lay the flicker inside. I filled in the hole and patted down the dirt. Then I did something unusual. Despite having buried dozens of animals in my life, this anonymous grave required something more—a marker. Spying an odd shard of splintered fiberglass under the shed, I drove one end into the grave. An inch or so showed above the ground. This wouldn't mean anything to anybody. Except me.

As much as we'd like—and regardless of our nurturing— we parents can't peer into the future. I don't know what decisions Indigo will make. Or what kind of person she'll become. Perhaps she'll cherish birds; perhaps she won't. I'm not sure I'd wish my bird interest—which borders on pathology—on anybody, for that matter. But if my daughter ends up noticing the little things, like an unfurling fern frond or the intricate patterns on a woodpecker's ruffled feathers, I'll be overjoyed indeed. I may even wander out back to this avian gravesite, to remember the bird interred within. In addition to increasing

Indigo's empathy, the unfortunate window collision may one day spark her interest, too. And from this interest, an enhanced life may burn—steadily and brightly—much more than merely a flicker.

5 · Birders Can't Ride Shotgun

The dominant primordial beast was strong in Buck, and under the fierce conditions of trail life it grew and grew. Yet it was a secret growth. His newborn cunning gave him poise and control.

—Jack London, *The Call of the Wild*

"So Ezra, when do you think we should—"

"White ibis!" Ezra shouted, pointing out my mother's window in Florida. I leaned forward on the couch and peered out. Sure enough, Ezra, then five years old, had found two pearly white ibis strolling through a neighbor's yard. As a fledgling parent, I was both annoyed and thrilled. Should I admonish him for interrupting my question, which I could now no longer remember? Or should I congratulate him for both finding and correctly naming one of Florida's most dazzling species? Before I could decide, his grandmother walked in and joined us at the window.

"I've been meaning to ask you what those white birds are." She sat down slowly to avoid spilling her coffee.

"They're actually white ibis, Grandmom!" Ezra peppered much of his speech with the word "actually." And he usually used it with a slightly know-it-all tone. Oh boy. So not only was my son interruptive. He was also pedantic. If any kid was going to get beat up at school, it was the know-it-all pedant with an overt fondness for "actually." Then again, I was partly proud, as

Ezra's grandmother had a vexing habit of calling every egret, stork, and ibis a "white bird" regardless of their innumerable differences. It drove me—and now Ezra—nuts.

While I would have loved to blame my wife's DNA for Ezra's behavior, I knew that mine was the more likely culprit. Through my daily behavior, I had shown Ezra that a man regularly interrupts a conversation to point out a bird, always corrects a wrongly named bird, and often slams on the brakes when a rare bird is spotted (many of these allegedly rare species have a pernicious habit of transforming into common ones upon closer inspection). Normally I do most of the driving. That way, when I see a "rare" bird, I can pull over. But when a rare bird shows up while Linda's at the wheel, I have modeled for Ezra that an otherwise sane man pounds on the dashboard and pleads to pull over. For safety and sanity, my urgent requests have been habitually ignored. When I can think straight, I credit Linda for her better judgment. And her tolerance. But when a rare bird is potentially afield, it's impossible to think straight. Muscles tense up. Neurons misfire. And odd and often puerile antics result.

This is why birders can't ride shotgun.

The problem may lie in a profound misunderstanding between birders and nonbirders. Nonbirders assume that birders go birding. They don't. Birders are birding. Always. Some of us—the less diehard—occasionally pause to sleep. As soon as we awaken, even before our eyes have opened, we're birding. Windows don't open merely for a breeze. Windows open for the dawn chorus. As soon as I'm fifty-one percent cognizant, I'm birding. Even though it may look to nonbirders like I'm cleaning the garage or staining the deck, I'm actually birding. And since I'm always birding, the opportunities to interrupt, correct, and annoy are omnipresent and endless.

I've periodically learned to temper my knack for noticing

everything avian. I forced it inside during my high school years when I feared my hobby wouldn't be deemed cool enough for my soccer-playing comrades. Several girlfriends were likewise none the wiser to my dual love interests. And the stress of grad school squashed it for a while. But with my diploma in hand and a job that includes teaching ornithology each year, the out-workings of my birdy brain have oozed back to the surface like an oil seep.

My decorum was tested again during a recent trip to the Everglades in Florida with my obliging parents. Wanting to get a sense for the sinuous rivers of grass, we departed for a two-hour boat tour from Flamingo Point. Since it was off-season and an odd midday hour, I shared the boat with about seven other folks, all of whom seemed normal enough. Although antsy to see great birds, I was resolved to appear as balanced and well-mannered as those around me. The tour started wonderfully. I kept my binoculars mostly lowered, made small talk with those around me, and laughed when the tour guide made unmemorable jokes about mangroves.

But then my façade fell away. Out of the corner of my eye, about thirty yards away, I saw an abnormal-looking mourning dove. Wait, that was no mourning dove; it was a white-crested pigeon! Knowing these birds were restricted to Florida's southern tip, I desperately wanted a better look at the bird that had now alighted atop a mangrove. I needed to be sure of my ID. More importantly, I needed to slow this darn boat down. My dilemma resurfaced. Should I try to stop the boat? Was it appropriate to hijack a general tour for a bird? Not just a bird, a pigeon. A pigeon! These pleasant-looking people would surely get mad. At least one would want me tossed to the gators.

Despite my resolve, my zeal exploded like fireworks. "White-crested pigeon!" I yelled, pointing off the starboard side. But the roaring engine reigned supreme. The skipper neither saw nor heard me. Or, more likely, he pretended not to. I'll never know. His large, dark sunglasses revealed nothing more than the requisite stoicism that comes with leading the same tour untold times a day for untold years. The other passengers heard me though. As did my parents. I sensed their normal parental pride dissipate as quickly as the pigeon did in my binoculars. Kindly, most of the others feigned interest with a curious nod or a sympathetic smile.

We finally slowed down next to a dense stand of trees that all looked like they were walking in the water. The skipper slowly unhooked the boat's microphone and in a remarkable monotone, taught us how to differentiate black and red mangroves. I felt cheated. He had passed over one of America's most geographically restricted birds—the white-crested pigeon—to robotically instruct us about adventitious roots?! Granted, mangroves were cool. But they registered far below birds on my biophilia meter. Next time, I vowed, this barge would brake for birds. I'd make sure of it.

Next time came just twenty minutes later. While speeding into a large lagoon, I saw a bird that was indisputably cool. He or she was perched high on a snag and looked downright debonair. A peregrine falcon. While not extremely rare, peregrines are always a treat to see. Especially this one, that appeared utterly apathetic to the noise of our boat's bombastic approach.

I glanced at the skipper. Like before, his face belied no emotion. Despite looking straight at the bird, he didn't seem to notice it. We weren't slowing down. What?! If anything we were speeding up. Still sore about the pigeon, I was not going to lose this peregrine. If we could halt our pleasure cruise for mangroves, alligators, and air plants, we had to stop for the fastest animal in the world, a bird that when clocked by Ken Franklin in 2005, hit 242 miles per hour.

Two hundred forty-two miles per hour! When Usain Bolt

hit his top speed of 27.8 miles per hour in Berlin, we gasped in awe and awarded an Olympic medal. The world reacted similarly to Secretariat's 49 miles per hour at the Belmont Stakes. Yes, speed is relative. But peregrine speed is relative and superlative. Everything about them is modified for it. Small, bony tubercles line the nostrils like inlet cones on jet engines. As air rushes in the nostrils it is slowed by rods and fins. These reduce the dramatic changes in air pressure and prevent lung damage, allowing the bird to breathe. An additional secretory gland prevents the corneas from drying out while a third eyelid—a nictitating membrane—spreads its tears and clears debris without sacrificing keen vision. The menacing dark markings around the eyes reduce glare. Keen vision and glare reduction is essential. Because peregrines don't just defy death, they inflict it during their miraculous stoops.

While the peregrine is falling like a meteorite, it's applying mathematical principles that would have impressed Pythagoras. Speed in a stoop is largely determined by drag coefficient. The lower the drag coefficient, the faster a falcon can free fall. Peregrines fold back their wings and tail, tuck their feet in, and drop. With a drag coefficient of 0.18, the crow-sized peregrine calculates exactly when to blast through the wing of an oblivious mallard, speeding along on its own trajectory at a cool sixty miles per hour. The peregrine slightly adjusts its tail and tucked-in primary feathers to alter its trajectory as it tracks its prey. The impact angle is critical; a direct hit can be suicidal. To live through an assault, a peregrine needs a glancing blow, which it makes with a clenched foot. A stunned, spiraling mallard is enough.

But the physiological feat isn't over yet. The falcon still has to slow its speed without ripping its wings off in the process. It accomplishes this with a U-shaped dive, gradually arcing upward, allowing gravity to slow it down. On the upswing, it uses its talons, now unclenched, to snatch the witless duck from the sky. If I were a mallard, I'd choose death by duck hawk. Alive one second, dead the next. Fast and furious.

But no. The skipper didn't see the falcon. My parents didn't see it. Nobody saw it. We had to see this!

I leapt up, gesticulated wildly, and shouted, "Peregrine falcon!" at the very top of my lungs. Weary heads snapped up all around me, obviously wondering why a binocular-toting lunatic had been allowed on board. No longer able to pretend he didn't see me, the skipper cupped his ear, indicating he couldn't hear me. I shouted again, stumbling into a railing as I did so. Ever so reluctantly, the skipper eased off the accelerator and grabbed the microphone.

"Folks," he said, somehow managing to sound both bored and annoyed, "we've got what our friend here calls an American falcon."

"A peregrine falcon!" I interrupted. "Peregrine!" I repeated more loudly. The captain ignored me.

"Yes, yes," he said again. "An American falcon. Oh look, there it goes," he added without a hint of disappointment, replacing the microphone in its holster on the dash. With a few strong, regal wingbeats, the peregrine lifted off and was soon a speck on the horizon. I couldn't blame it. I would leave, too, if I had been called an American falcon despite having a geographic range that spans the globe.

The skipper pushed back the throttle and I lurched back to my seat. Too embarrassed to make eye contact with even my parents, I stared off into south Florida's shimmering water that looked decidedly less tranquil than it had when the trip started. I was defeated. If I was the skipper of this boat, I concluded grumpily, I'd brake for birds and call them by their proper names. Whether in a car or on a boat, riding shotgun was painful indeed.

In the midst of my self-righteous stupor, I noticed a line of beautiful white birds soaring some fifty yards off the bow. I lifted off my seat but hastily forced myself back down. No. Not this time.

I wasn't going to shout it out to my fellow passengers. I'd annoyed enough people for one day. Yes, I was always birding. That didn't mean I had to force others to do so, too. After all, even I had been annoyed by my son's interruptive and pedantic insistence on accurate avian nomenclature. If the other passengers saw the beautiful white birds and enjoyed them—great. If they didn't, they didn't. But Ezra and I surely wished that everybody on this blasted boat knew one final thing. Yes, these were white birds. But actually—and far more satisfyingly—they were white ibis.

Surf scoter

6 · CHOMPING AT NATURE'S BIT

Nature does not hurry, yet everything is accomplished.

—Lao Tzu

A surf scoter is a large black diving sea duck that I rarely get a chance to see as an inland-dwelling western New Yorker. So when I heard of one resting on a water body about an hour away in Batavia, New York, I brainstormed some errands I could accomplish after a nice quick look at my first scoter. What an easy bird to add to my life list, I thought, as I pulled into Batavia's water treatment facility. Especially compared to the nonbreeding shorebirds I often sought that all seemed to be ever so slight permutations of one another, distinguished literally by shades of gray. But the surf scoter would be a slam dunk. Its boldly patterned head had earned it a colloquial name, the "skunk-headed coot." The bird should prove easy to find and even easier to ascertain. I'd be home in a jiffy.

I was right on the first count. The bird proved remarkably easy to find. It bobbed like an ebony-colored buoy completely alone in one of the facility's impoundments. Smiling widely, I lowered my truck window and raised my binoculars. This was fast and easy bird finding at its finest. I focused my binoculars. Magnified ten times, the scoter looked big and black and . . . headless. The bird, either cold or sleepy or both, had its head tucked so deeply into its coverts I could barely decipher its breast from its rump.

Lots of birds are identifiable without a head. Blue jays, robins, goldfinches—all these birds have irrelevant heads to a busy birder. Not so with scoters. A headless scoter is as useful as a wheel-less wheelbarrow. Akin to trying to distinguish a fish crow from an American crow on a moonless night. My scoter, which my Internet listserv had claimed was a surf scoter, could be a black or a white-winged scoter. I needed to see the head.

I lowered my binoculars and reclined my seat. This was no reason to panic. I'd wait. Sea ducks can't sleep forever.

But, it slowly dawned on me, they can. Especially headless ones. My alleged surf scoter had no respect for the endless items on my to-do list. It remained as inert as a noble gas. After ten minutes of staring and not getting any errands accomplished, I grew antsy. So antsy in fact that I broke a code of conduct I've long held. Simply put, I don't interfere with nature unless absolutely necessary. Yes, I immerse myself in it. I enjoy it in many ways. But unless it's for teaching purposes, I don't disrupt it. I like to think of myself as respectfully seated in the balcony when witnessing wildlife dramas, not crinkling candy wrappers in the front row.

But this statuesque scoter had me beaten. I was exasperated. I opened my door and slammed it. Certainly no sleepy scoter could ignore such a gunshot-like sound.

This scoter, however, was an exception to the norm. Its head remained as buried as a Devonian fossil. I opened and slammed the door again. Again. And again. Now I was sounding like a semi-automatic. Still nothing. Either this scoter was stone deaf, had earplugs jammed in its auriculars, or it hailed from downtown Los Angeles.

I looked at my watch. I had to get a vacuum cleaner fixed. If I didn't buy a garden fence today, our marauding groundhogs might call all their friends for the free buffet. Moreover, I had kids. I was always needed at home. The sand in the hourglass was falling swiftly. For all I knew, this scoter could sleep like this until nightfall. I couldn't take it anymore. My code of conduct now in shreds, I climbed out of my truck. I slammed my hands on the roof and then, like the scoter, lost my own head. With primeval, hairsplitting yells, I shouted at the scoter and began a series of angry, wild-eyed jumping jacks.

In the midst of my Neanderthal-like madness, I didn't see the blue sedan until it pulled right up behind me.

Mortified, I tried to transform my witless histrionics into a well-calculated yoga stretch. But nobody in his right mind shouts while doing meditative yoga in a wastewater treatment plant. I had to patch out. I dove into my truck, slammed the door one final time out of spite, and sped away, too embarrassed to glance in my rearview mirror. I drove home skunked by the skunk-headed coot. And try as I have to forget it, my scoter humiliation has resurfaced time and again whenever I've found myself chomping at nature's bit.

I downright drowned in this memory, for example, when I recently uncovered a quote by Ralph Waldo Emerson. "Adopt the pace of nature," Emerson penned nearly two centuries ago, "her secret is patience." It's a palpable irony that makes me grimace. Why? Because patience, I've found in my hectic life as a perpetually behind college professor, routinely proves the most elusive of virtues. But I know Emerson had the magic word. Whenever and wherever I've been truly patient in nature, I've been rewarded.

Of all the nature partakers out there, perhaps it's hunters who understand this the most. Especially the ones who sit out in a blind each autumn. If you ever take the time to ask a hunter what they saw during their dawn-to-dusk vigils they often spend in the woods, you'll recognize a recurrent theme. Long bouts of stillness interrupted with wondrous spectacles. Chickadees that land on gun barrels. Cooper's hawks that capture flickers in split-second flights. Porcupines that nibble shoelaces. I even had one hunter (not known for hyperbole) tell me how a red fox sat on his hand for a few seconds and, after realizing its error, vanished like a wraith. Nature moves in punctuated equilibrium. Unlike nature documentaries that compress years of footage into a half-hour, real nature observation has long intermissions between dramatic acts. If you're lucky enough—and patient enough—to witness a dramatic act in real time, it will sear the memory like a hot iron.

At my stage of life, I have to cultivate patience with intentionality. It's far easier not to, of course. I found an opportunity when the most observant member of my family, Willow, then ten months old, discovered—and naturally tried to eat—a gorgeous green luna moth that she found in a dusty corner by the sink.

All three of my kids gathered around the recently deceased moth. Other than a slight bird nibble out of one wing, it was intact. Whatever funeral we gave it, this beauty deserved an open casket. The trashcan seemed far too undignified. No, we would scatter the moth to the winds, knowing any number of scavengers would soon delight in this well-preserved, dense package of protein. But first, to fix the spectacle into our own memories, we would paint pictures of it. If any act slows us down and cultivates patience, it is the production of art.

On a little plastic table under a maple tree out front, we ceremoniously spread our supplies around the moth. No masterpiece was going to be produced under these conditions, however. Ezra "accidentally" sprayed us with the hose. Indigo kept bumping the table. And Willow kept trying to eat the paint tubes. But for a few precious moments, we studied the moth and painted our own pictures. And in so doing, we felt the breeze, heard an indigo bunting, and failed to find a shade of green that truly matched the luna's natural patina.

I'd be lying to say we adopted the pace of nature. But I do believe our corporate compass pointed that way. I'm realistic enough to know that even the cultivation of patience requires patience. Due to our vigil under the maple, maybe my kids will remember the day we found a luna in the house. And what a luna looks like as it blows around an art table.

At the very least, I'm hoping that if any of my kids ever find themselves trying to identify a headless scoter, they'll be dignified about it. And that they'll each maintain a well-developed and respectful code of conduct with the natural world. One in which they'll appreciate seeing a scoter, regardless of what species it is. Nature's secret, as Emerson wrote, is patience. It rarely rewards those who rush. Most of the time, adopting the pace of nature is the only way to get ahead. And it's definitely the only way to get a head you desperately need for proper identification.

Cock-of-the-rock

7 · THE BIRDS AND THE BEES

Dressing up is a bore. At a certain age, you decorate yourself to attract the opposite sex, and at a certain age, I did that. But I'm past that age.

—Katharine Hepburn

Every kid learns about sex in their own way. I am a case in point. As is true for many kids growing up in the country, a cow pasture formed the border of my backyard. When my friends and I weren't daring each other to pee on the electric fence, we tended to ignore the bucolic behemoths that placidly ignored us in kind.

But one spring morning, I could not ignore my lazy, life-long neighbors. Glancing out the window, I noticed a large bull that seemed to be pushing a smaller, wide-eyed cow across the field like a wheelbarrow. The bull completed several lascivious laps around the pasture with his concubine before falling off with an exasperated bellow.

Like lots of coming-of-age kids, I was both curious and confused. The tryst did not seem consensual. But each time the female outran her amorous assailant, she'd stop and wait for him to remount. Not knowing what would happen next, I remained where I was, transfixed by this unexpected cattle concupiscence. I never heard my father behind me until he spoke.

"They're having sex," he remarked dryly. As the bull remounted and the wheelbarrow routine resumed, my dad couldn't resist adding a few more titillating aphorisms, bespeaking his rural Tennessee roots. Mercifully, he left for work before I could respond and reveal any further embarrassment. This episode, which felt more like a low-budget beer commercial, was my first lesson about sex. And I obviously never forgot it.

Now with young children of my own, I jealously applaud my father's straightforward, opportunistic approach to sex education. I share his style, I've learned, but lack his gumption. And since I also lack a pasture out back, I've harbored a cattle-less conundrum about the best way to proceed with my own offspring.

Figuring that water is purest at its source, I turned first to the sex doctor himself, Sigmund Freud. But of all Freud's writings on sex, it was an unrelated quote that struck me the deepest: "When inspiration fails to come to me," Freud wrote, "I go halfway to meet it."

My halfway ended up being pretty far: the foothills of the Andes Mountains in Ecuador. But as Freud predicted, inspiration did indeed meet me, arriving five minutes after I settled down with a dozen of my bleary-eyed college students at a well-known lek, a place where male birds regularly display for females in hopes of landing a mate. We were after one particular bird—the cock-of-the-rock—that has drawn birders from time immemorial. One Andean cock-of-the-rock would have sufficed. We found a half-dozen. The fantastical, blaze-orange birds bobbed their heads and riotously sang as if their lives depended on it. Because that's just it, we slowly realized, their lives did depend on it.

Everything about the cock-of-the-rock, as with the cattle I'd observed decades before, was predicated on procreation. Pseudo-scholar or not, Freud rightly theorized that sex drives life. Charles Darwin coined the term sexual selection, a force dictating survival as powerfully as his more famous concept, natural selection. At its simplest, sexual selection is nothing more than discerning females choosing the most beautiful—or the fittest—males. Victorian culture wasn't ready for Darwin's ideas. Sexual selection gave too much power to women, so Darwin—and his 898-page monograph on the subject—was politely ignored.

But culture changed and as it did, a slew of other scientists put Darwin's cockamamie theory to the test. They hacked tails off some birds, glued extensions on others, and painted various plumages. Then they did things meddling scientists typically do, assiduously numbering nests, measuring mating attempts, and enumerating eggs. Details differed but the synopsis was the same. In short, female birds love fashion, novelty, and extravagance. In the animal kingdom, crazy long tails, a cacophony of colors, and a jumbled assortment of other doodads are downright arresting to the lady folk; the more otherworldly the outfit and the more dazzling the display, the more smitten the ladies become.

"The sight of a feather in a peacock's tail," Darwin once lamented, "makes me sick." But later, in the light of lovemaking, its reasons became clear. True, a male peacock's train, toting over 150 elaborate eyespots, makes little sense to the story of survival. But in the story of sex, eyespots are billboards for health and vigor. You can't be loaded down with parasites, for example, if you're flitting about the forest in an ostentatious overcoat.

Unsurprisingly, the cock-of-the-rock first caught my attention due to its name alone (juvenile humor may fade but it never disappears entirely). I quickly learned, however, that cocks-of-the-rocks, if that is indeed how you pluralize this bird, are not the worst offenders. Seemingly every bird we encountered in the tropics, and even some in my native state of New York, was in some sense surreal with equally superlative names.

Watching species like the beryl-spangled tanager, long-tailed sylph, and flame-faced tanager, almost required sunglasses. To females, these glittering gems are dreamy. Now educated in Freud and Darwin, I can only imagine how a female booby's heart must flutter when she looks licentiously upon her consort's powdery blue feet.

There in the morning mist, I realized my students were grasping the power of sex on species survival as memorably as I did so many years back with my convenient cow pasture. So I channeled my father's opportunism. "What about humans?" I asked my students once we'd left the lek. "Surely sexual selection doesn't act upon us?"

A pause.

Then, sure as a black-tailed trainbearer's tail, the comments came. Tanning, high heels, bodybuilding, nose jobs, extreme dieting, hair dyes, make-up, enhancements, reductions, Botox . . . We're so steeped in sexual selection we've almost ceased to see it. For our species, it's less clear who's dressing up for whom, and who's doing the choosing. Nuances aside, the many multi-billion dollar industries that result from Darwin's simple theory are testament to its unparalleled presence and power.

Despite clichés that warn me against it, I continue to—at least initially—judge books by their covers. But watching tanagers and trainbearers has exposed me to double standards I didn't know I had. Although I like to think otherwise, I'm just as susceptible to preening and prancing. So I've resolved to change. Not cataclysmically, of course. Enough to make me opt for spending thirty minutes on a walk instead of the weight room, veering away from these many-mirrored rooms devoted to vanity. More importantly, I've learned that lots of human nature is as brainless as the backyard cows I once watched.

No, I don't have the luxury of a pasture out back to educate my son about sex. But I've got a creek, a forest, a whole ecosystem.

For learning about the birds and the bees, we'll have to forgo cows. And I think we'll leave the bees alone, too. I'm not worried. As I learned in Ecuador, the birds will more than suffice.

8 · SEARCHING FOR A LANDSCAPE IDENTITY

For a relationship with landscape to be lasting, it must be reciprocal.

—Barry Lopez

"Great gray owl!" my son, Ezra, shouted from the backseat. I hit the brakes and pulled over, Ezra and I craning our necks out the side windows.

"Nope." I lowered my binoculars. "Barred owl."

"Gimme your bins, Dad!" Ezra demanded, his absence of manners almost as troubling as his incredulity. I glanced at him in the rearview mirror. Here was a scientist—a born skeptic—squeezed into a nine-year-old body. "Guess you're right," he conceded, handing back my binoculars.

We were slightly deflated. Granted, any owl was cool. But we were after a great gray, undisputed Zeus of the owl pantheon. Although exceedingly rare, we had expected a great gray here in this nondescript meadow in the mountains of southern Oregon. Why? For a simple reason: I had seen one here before.

Other birders have confessed they share in my suffering. It's a common, yet chronic, disease. The symptoms are straightforward but the cure, if there is one, isn't. It goes like this: If you see something cool, the next time out—perhaps even years later—you expect to see it where you did that first time. My particular manifestation of this odd, nature-lover affliction is even worse. I often expect to see what I've seen before not only in the same tree, but perched on the very same limb.

Species themselves are partly to blame. Some exhibit, in the lingo of behaviorists, strong site fidelity, otherwise known as philopatry. Derived from the Greek, meaning "home-loving," philopatric critters are loyal to localities. Some megapodes, or ground-laying birds, in Australia, for example, will reuse the same mound for a nest every year, only abandoning it when calamity strikes or it literally falls down around them. That's breeding-site philopatry. Another form, natal philopatry, is living out your years where you were raised. This coming-back-to-our-roots is the form most of us can relate to. It also explains my particular fondness for a pair of phoebes that faithfully chooses the same eave under my porch year after year after year. When this pair passes on, I'm confident their kids or grandkids will take over. They're attached and so am I.

But nature is varied. Many other species refuse to don such straitjackets. When they're not manacled to a nest or frantically feeding fledglings, they're prone to wander widely. Others are more nomadic, dyed-in-the-wool vagabonds—the human equivalent of our wanderlust friends that head west in their vintage Volkswagen camper vans. I understand all this. Even so, each day I drive home from work, I scan the same snag or ditch or fencepost, hoping for the same owl or hawk or meadowlark that I saw once before. Rain or snow, if my friends aren't where they're supposed to be, I'm let down. But hope springs eternal and tomorrow I'll scan the exact same places again.

Part of the problem is that the roots of this see-it-once-expect-to-see-it-again condition are buried in a spot that's only accessible to a brain surgeon: the medial temporal lobe of the hippocampus. This vast neuronal network is the wardrobe in which our mental maps and memories are hung. When we revisit a place where we experienced something memorable—say, saw a great gray owl—the place cells in the hippocampus fire anew. As Jennifer Ackerman writes in *The Genius of Birds*, our memory of a thought is married to the place where it first happened.

This is why, I'm guessing, many birders I know are as philopatric as some of the species they search for. We birders pay attention. Consciously or not, we're perpetually scanning: tree limbs, rooflines, hilltops. We study contours, scrutinize specks, and look for irregularity. Usually we find nothing. Occasionally, lightning strikes. And when it does, and that irregularity turns into a great gray owl, it's satisfying in the same way that finding your lost car keys is, provided they're in a spot you've already looked twelve times, of course. Over time, our well of memorable sightings deepens and our connection to place—our place—grows stronger. Certainly the lure of watching bountiful birds in exotic locales is ever enticing. But my circle of birder friends agree with Dorothy: there's no place like home.

These feelings form, in the words of psychologist Ferdinando Fornara and his Italian research team, a landscape identity. For Fornara, this identity includes "a set of memories, conceptions, interpretations, and feelings related to a specific physical setting." It goes like this: The more time we spend in an area, the stronger the bond. Everybody that lives in a place for a while develops some sort of landscape identity. Seems pretty obvious. Less obvious, perhaps, is my guess that birders—and surely botanists, lepidopterists, and all stripes of nature lovers—form stronger landscape identities than others. Why? Because it's not only the birds we grow fond of. The habitat that housed the birds—the swamps, brush piles, and power lines—becomes just as wonderful. Because of this, birders and other nature-lovers can find beauty in places others can't.

This is why I wasn't too surprised when I saw a house advertised recently on an online birding listserv. It was near, but not on, Lake Ontario. Rather than lakefront with expansive views, this house was across the street, its view obstructed by other houses, fences, and hedges. "Great house and migratory stopover site," the ad read. "Rarities not uncommon." Despite the oxymoronic last line, the house undoubtedly lived up to its billing. Every spring and fall, songbirds, intimidated or exhausted by the Great Lake, probably dropped by in droves. The birds didn't need waterfront and limitless views. They wanted brushy tangles, hedges, and swampy areas, places with food. The advertised house was one refined aesthetes with deep wallets would scoff at. Quite literally, it was a house for the birds. And since it was, the savvy house lister went after birders.

System administrators promptly removed the listing, which didn't surprise me either. It was a site for listing birds, not houses. Regrettably, I wasn't able to read the fine print before the ad was pulled. Perhaps it was an opportunistic birder who needed to sell the house quickly. I can't help but hope on a deeper level that the house seller and I are the same species, one with a stronger-than-usual landscape identity, made even stronger by the great birds that we can't keep ourselves from searching for.

Just around the bend from where I spent my childhood summers in Pennsylvania lies a bucolic township of rolling fields called Brooklyn. This Brooklyn, with less than 1,000 people, couldn't be more different from its outsized bigger brother. It's iconic farm country with little notoriety except for one thing: Actor Richard Gere grew up there. Once or twice a summer, my dad took me out to breakfast intentionally swinging by Brooklyn on the way home. And every time he did, his line was the same. "Richard Gere grew up here, you know." I nodded and smiled, looking out my side window as if expecting to catch the Golden Globe Award winner out on a tractor. Gere only occasionally visits Brooklyn nowadays. But even so, he lends the otherwise anonymous map dot a certain cachet.

The presence of a ruffed grouse does the same. Renowned ecologist Aldo Leopold once wrote: "Everybody knows that the autumn landscape in the northwoods is the land, plus a red maple, plus a ruffed grouse. In terms of conventional physics, the grouse represents only a millionth of either the mass or the energy of an acre. Yet, subtract the grouse and the whole thing is dead."

Leopold was writing about more than mere ecological equations. He was expounding on the importance of that slippery concept called value—subjective value of landscape—and the importance of cryptic little chicken-like birds. Granted, tourists will never flock to the north woods to gape at coveys of grouse teetering about the underbrush. Leopold knew that. He also knew that grouse aren't even vital for ensuring ecological function (helpful, yes, but not essential). He was after intrinsic value. That grouse are there, even if rarely glimpsed, is what counts.

I learned this lesson early and in an unexpected way. The movie Jaws played on our old, boxy TV in the family room. My nerve-wracked, eight-year-old frame was wedged between my two older siblings. Like millions of other viewers, I was terrified. Not whenever the great white appeared, but, rather, when it didn't. When it lurked below, John Williams's infamous score launched me into apoplexy. Two-thirds of the film, the shark is submerged, shrouded in mystery.

It was a happy accident. Spielberg disliked the sharks he'd commissioned. They weren't frightening enough. With time running out, he opted to keep his great white concealed. It was pragmatic, Hitchcockian, and genius. Jaws quickly became the highest grossing movie in US history, winning three Academy Awards and spawning musicals, theme park rides, and best-selling computer games. More importantly, it showed us all that the mere idea of a shark is more mesmerizing than the shark itself.

I'm convinced that birders, and most other nature enthusiasts for that matter, understand this idea. What we have trouble understanding, however, are attempts that scholars sometimes make to quantify such value. In 2016, Fornara and his cadre of researchers, the same folks who coined "landscape identity," attempted to quantify the subjective value people have toward place. It was a simple experiment: photographs of natal and foreign landscapes were placed in front of subjects who were asked to evaluate their feelings of "self" in response. Unsurprisingly, photos of one's native region tended to produce stronger emotions. Yes, the researchers dryly concluded, research lent some quantitative support to the theory of landscape identity.

Something about the act of objectifying subjective feelings doesn't sit right. In my graduate seminars, I well remember my distinguished professors cogently arguing about the need for attaching dollar signs to ecosystems and the services they freely render. As a professor myself, I've assigned heavy-duty readings on the subject, like "Economic Reasons for Conserving Wild Nature," which appeared in Science not too long ago. The logic is straightforward. Humanity benefits from nature. Such benefits should incentivize us to conserve it. But they don't. The benefits we enjoy from ecosystems are difficult to commoditize, making them even more difficult to capture with conventional, market-based analysis. So humanity continues to convert habitat—a euphemism for destroying it—relentlessly.

My desire to affix price tags on the world's ecosystems is tempered by the chilling words of Kenyan Nobel Peace Prize winner Wangari Maathai, who founded Kenya's Greenbelt

Movement. "If you can sell it," Maathai wrote, "you can forget about protecting it." She had witnessed a trend as Kenya transitioned from a colonial state to independence. Privatizing public land, or commoditizing it in any way, ended in habitat conversion and development. Landscape identities were converted in the process; some were lost entirely. Attaching dollar signs to nature is a two-edged sword. And in some places, it cuts both ways.

A few months ago, I walked into an information kiosk for the Cascade-Siskiyou National Monument in southern Oregon. The tiny kiosk appeared to be a converted tool shed. September sunlight streamed through the lone window as I browsed the displays. On my way out, a poster by the door caught my eye. "WHY YOU SHOULD CARE ABOUT BUTTERFLIES," it proclaimed in big, block lettering. Underneath in smaller print were a host of services the butterflies provided, from pollination to pest control.

I commend the intentions of such poster makers. But it worries me, too. Is it another misguided attempt to put objective value on subjective, priceless things? More worrisome, of course, is that we need reasons to care in the first place.

Native Americans certainly didn't need reasons to care. Nor do they today. Recognizing that the land is the source of all sustenance, it has long been the de facto definer of identity, both tribally and individually. Leslie Marmon Silko, a Laguna Pueblo writer, suggests the term "landscape" is misleading, namely how it has entered the English language. A landscape is not a portion of territory the eye can comprehend in a single view. Nor does it correctly encompass the relationship between humans and their surroundings. Viewers are not outside or separate. Rather, Silko writes, "viewers are as much a part of the landscape as the boulders they stand on." Likewise,

Luther Standing Bear, Chief of the Oglala Sioux, saw precious little separation between humans and nature. "The American Indian is of the soil," he wrote, "whether it be in the region of forests, plains, pueblos, or mesas. He fits into the landscape, for the hand that fashioned the continent also fashioned man for his surroundings. He belongs just as the buffalo belonged."

My doctoral advisor drove this home to me while in a very different context, one that also stands much to lose if people are viewed outside of nature. I was ready to launch a five-year study of human-wildlife interactions along the edges of Serengeti National Park, in Tanzania. To kick off the project, scientists of all stripes convened in the Park for a biocomplexity conference. At the end of the meeting, one of the principle investigators of the large grant that had gotten us here introduced me as a grad student who was going to be working at the interface between the human and natural worlds. Dramatically, he drew an X on the whiteboard and pointed to the middle of it—the intersection of the two lines. "Right here," he said, pausing for emphasis, "is where one of our students will be working." I gulped, both overwhelmed and honored. That student was me. My face tomato red, I dutifully copied the diagram into my small notebook, writing the word "me" in the middle of the X. The letter X now indicated far more than buried treasure; it represented the next few years of my life.

After the meeting, we rode back to our lodge on a small minibus. With the bus in motion along a bumpy park road, my advisor slipped out of her seat in front and slid towards the back next to me. She looked at me, frowning. "Did you take notes on that meeting?"

"Yes," I said, somewhat proudly. Such a good student I was, taking notes.

"Let me see it."

I fished the notebook out of my pocket. She grabbed it,

turned to the page with the copied diagram, and scribbled it out. In its place she drew a circle and wrote two words in the middle. "Humans" and "nature." "Things can't meet if they aren't apart in the first place." She handed back my notebook. "It's all one system."

I've never forgotten that simple lesson. Rather than spending my remaining days on earth trying to convince people why they should care about the natural world, I prefer to teach this lesson—we're all in this together. Caring may be irrelevant anyway. "It doesn't matter whether people care or don't care," says science writer Elizabeth Kolbert. "What matters is that people change the world."

Placing ourselves in nature is critical. It's the only way to recognize our reciprocal relationship. And it's my rationale for spending my days immersing people in the natural world, be they my children, my students, and even my parents. Instead of trying to drum up reasons to care, I've decided to invest in forming landscape identities. It's a small goal, but it seems more attainable. I focus on birds, although butterflies and flowers work too. Birds are bountiful (for now at least), beautiful, and pretty easy to get attached to. With a little practice, one can figure out where to find them. Sometimes, of course, they come to us.

But on that afternoon drive in the mountains of southern Oregon, the owl we sought—the great gray—hadn't come to us. Like always I had irrationally expected it on the same limb as before. This owl lived above the trammels of routine. Reluctantly, we said goodbye to the meadow and drove on. Thirty seconds later, I brought our car to a screeching halt. There, on a skinny fencepost a stone's throw away, was an impossibly large and regal bird. It was so obvious that even my skeptical son didn't need to confirm it. The great gray owl swiveled its massive head and leered at us with lemon-yellow eyes. We snapped photos, looked through binoculars, and watched. It dawned on me then that we'd found much more than an owl. We'd found a point of attachment. We'd found, each in our own way, the start of a landscape identity.

I've never seen another great gray owl. Since I no longer live in the mountains of southern Oregon, it's unlikely I ever will again. That's okay. I know the sunny glades where they hunt and the shadowy haunts they retire to. I know they're out there, hidden from human eyes. Perching. Pouncing. Priceless.

9 · The Nature of Nature

To keep every cog and wheel is the first precaution of intelligent tinkering.

—Aldo Leopold

I recently endured three days of an enflamed, itchy hand. Even worse was the subsequent aversion of my daughter. I could choose from several scapegoats. But I'm laying the blame on a spotted owl.

"Daddy, will you scratch my back?" six-year-old Indigo asked, flopping onto her stomach on her bed. "But please don't use your yucky swollen hand!" Frowning, I obliged, scratching with my right hand while hiding my scary left hand behind my back. Our nighttime ritual complete, I walked down the stairs thinking about my daughter's revulsion to my most recent gift from nature: a nasty sting from a yellow jacket.

Such a sting was nothing new for me. Nor were any of the maladies nature routinely bestowed me, be it poison ivy, sunburn, or even my recent bout with Lyme disease. What was new was Indigo's aversion. Yes, my lipstick-colored hand was hard to look at. The knuckles had disappeared and it looked as if I had inflated my hand with helium. Why Indigo's odd reaction this time? Perhaps, I mused, it was the way I incurred the sting.

Which again, has to be the fault of a spotted owl. The bird is used to getting blamed and pulled into things it didn't—and doesn't—deserve. The reclusive owl has become an icon, thrust into the spotlight in the 1980s, emblemizing the value struggle in conservation. It isn't alone. Other species like the bald eagle, the snail darter, and even the Kihansi spray toad have had their day in the limelight. But the story of the spotted owl seems somehow different. Perhaps because everybody, from Winnie-the-Pooh lovers to Harry Potter and Guardians of Ga'Hoole fans, have a soft spot for owls. The fact that the spotted owl happens to have a hankering for mighty, old-growth trees surely plays a role as well. The most likely reason for the raging controversy, however, is that the two sides have historically appeared so simple: right versus wrong, stewardship versus greed, good versus evil. Good were the owls in their old-growth roosts. Evil were the timber barons hell-bent on profit. All traces of helpful nuance disappeared as rapidly as the owl's habitat. Even today, the controversy is a pitiful caricature: smoke-belching bulldozers versus weepy tree-huggers. The reality of the situation was far different. It is far different. And context, as they say, is everything.

Despite living in the right habitat in southern Oregon, I had long since given up the idea of seeing a wild spotted owl. Even in the best of circumstances, it's a low-density, shy, nocturnal bird that prefers gloomy, hard-to-access real estate. The bigger the trees the better, a view the owl unfortunately shares with the timber industry seeking maximum return on investment. But as often is the case, economically sound logic can be ecologically tragic. While I had little hope of seeing the owl, I did have firm plans for good, old-fashioned commensalism.

In biological lingo, a commensal species benefits from another without harming it. That was my intention. Yet for me the bar was even lower. I didn't need to lay eyes on an owl. Or interact with it in any way. I needed only to hang out where it lived. The owl's existence somewhere in the surrounding forest was enough. For my daughter Indigo, who loves to draw, a sketchbook and crayons were enough. What better way to spend an afternoon, I reasoned, than to create some art with my daughter in a nearby old-growth forest?

So we did just that, sketching plants and birds while we listened to the creak and groan of the primeval trees around us. Was a spotted owl listening to our banter from some far off, lichen-encrusted perch? In the magisterial habitat we were in, I hoped so. Even if not, the small, dark-eyed owl leered out from my imagination. This enriched the moment immeasurably, affirming the owl's intrinsic value.

Sometime later, our pictures finished, we headed out on a different path. Unfortunately, this path held a cantaloupe-sized yellow jacket nest hanging low on an understory limb. It was too late when I noticed it. "Run, Indigo!" I yelled, seeing the agitated cluster of angry wasps. Run she did. To my relief, she escaped unscathed. I nearly did, too, except for my left hand holding our supplies.

It was a typical sting that followed the usual sequence: pain, swelling, itchiness. I awoke a few times that night scratching. And had trouble typing and closing my hand throughout. But it was gone in a week. No big deal. Indigo, however, was entranced from the moment after the sting and charted my progress like a dutiful nurse. She seemed to be charting more than mere symptoms. Methodically, she was assessing nature. Or, more specifically, the nature of nature: its gifts, its demands, even its sheer whimsy. With me as the test subject, she had watched nature extend her hand benevolently and then, without warning, withdraw it. And now she was charting my reaction.

My reaction, of course, was mixed. I loathe stinging insects. And if anybody other than an entomologist claims otherwise, they're lying. Just like I loathe stinging nettle, poison ivy, and all manner of ticks. I admit I'd like to rid the planet of all these vile creatures once and for all. Fortunately, a smidgeon of logic anchors my ship. I understand food chains and the importance of holding onto every rivet for keeping our ecological airplane in the sky. We need every strand of silk in our food web. And every pollinator we can get.

Alas, I'm no John Muir. Yes, the mountains are calling and I must go. But I'll load my pack with bug spray and never pretend to like yellow jackets. So I didn't hide my mixed reaction from Indigo. I showed her my nonchalant, it's-no-big-deal approach. I also showed her what periodic outbursts about satanic insects sound like. I strived for stoicism but failed, all mind over matter until I'd break down, muttering unmentionables while shamelessly scratching my enflamed hand. Through it, Indigo clearly saw my unequal love for the world's creatures. I value them all, yes. But could happily do without a lot of them, too. There are double standards in such an approach. My hypocrisy, however, is hopefully buoyed by honesty. I may not like every species. But I like nature. Love it, even. So goes, I hope, the beauty of a nuanced view.

What does this have to do with a spotted owl? Well, everything, in fact. The spotted owl story is far more complex than what it's been reduced to: longtime logging families and the timber industry against conservation-minded West Coasters. The innards of the debate require sound ecological research and a heavy dose of ethics. Here's what we know: From 1985-2013, spotted owls dropped by eighty percent in some parts of the Pacific Northwest. Alarmed, the US Forest Service created the "Northwest Forest Plan," which limited logging on most of the 24.5 million designated acres of public land in Oregon, Washington, and Northern California. The plan protected about one thousand terrestrial and aquatic species in old-growth ecosystems.

But the shy and seductive spotted owl lay at its heart.

Lest the corks fly off the champagne bottles too soon, we should acknowledge a complicating fact. Yes, conservation-minded West Coasters may have the moral high ground. Opting for the long-term intrinsic value of owls over the shorter-term instrumental value of timber, paper products, and profit, is hard to dispute. But the high ground itself may be seismically unstable. The eighty percent decrease in spotted owls wasn't entirely due to the timber industry. At least it hasn't been lately. Part of the decline may be due to competition from another charismatic species, the barred owl. The barred owl looks identical to the spotted except for one minor wardrobe adjustment. Instead of spots on its chest, it sports attractive filigree barring.

As with so many other ecological problems, we've made this one ourselves. By chopping down so much old-growth before the Plan got underway, barred owls, adaptable colonizers that they are, moved right in, displacing spotted owls in the process. Calling barred owls adaptable colonizers, however, is sugarcoating them too much. They're imperialistic, often outright bullies. Researcher David Wiens of the US Geological Survey put radio tags on twenty-nine spotted owls and twenty-eight barred owls in western Oregon. Then he conducted espionage, tracking their every move. The slightly bigger, more aggressive barred owls proved too irksome for the deferential spotteds. The closer that barred owls lived to spotted, the less likely the spotted were to bear young. They couldn't procreate in a thin-walled apartment. Barred owls, however, couldn't care less. The more the merrier. Two to three pairs of barred owls hung out in territories that used to be claimed by just one pair of spotted owls.

A conservation conundrum like this offers one obvious but morally questionable solution—kill the barred owls. After a long and tendentious debate, the US Fish and Wildlife Service concluded exactly that. Killing one morally valuable species for another, essentially disposing one owl for another, can't be done lightly. Ethicist William Lynn, a researcher with the George Perkins Marsh Institute, sanctioned the Fish and Wildlife decision, but not without serious reservation. "We can't kill our way back to biodiversity," Lynn stated. ". . . In the long run, restoring habitat and finding non-lethal alternatives is the only ethical answer."

Here is an ethicist—a conservationist—conceding to short-term, albeit questionable techniques for problems that ultimately require long-term, sound management strategies. I haven't met William Lynn but I can't help but like him, especially his honesty. He realizes we're in a fix and his mind seems open. If anybody understands the importance of ethics, he does. He also knows that all our values can't always line up. Some of the most important decisions in conservation can't be made without serious reservations.

It's impossible to live life, I've found, without difficult value judgments. Ecological problems are too complicated to allow for monolithic, bumper sticker viewpoints. There aren't just two sides to everything; sometimes there are three sides, or even four. Context, while often difficult to dig up, always needs exhuming. In some spatial and temporal contexts, instrumental values—and the management strategies that spring from them—are sufficient and fine. In others, like the owl's, management has to act upon intrinsic value, one that's hard to commoditize. This is why I blame the spotted owl. It oozes intrinsic value. The coolness factor is clutched way too tightly in its talons. Its brooding charismatic aura is akin to other shy, mysterious species like the mountain gorilla and the snow leopard. Yet it packs all this irreplaceable intrinsic value in a much smaller, 3.6-pound frame.

Some people refuse to recognize such value. Others are ambivalent. And then there's me; hopelessly drawn in, content to hang out in the owl's haunts. When it comes to valuing nature, I've seen my hypocrisy and double standards pop up. Even so, the spotted owl is worth it. So too are the barred owl and the yellow jackets. All species are. But all species are also different. Some are common; some are rare. Some are retiring; some are brazen. Some defend themselves; some need our defense. All these differences add up to one thing: how we go about conserving each one has to differ too.

My hope is that even after my influence has diminished, Indigo will also think the spotted owl is worth it. I hope she'll discover that it's okay if she can't always align her values. And that even the best ethical approach sometimes comes with misgivings. Two things she knows already: The safest path is hard to discern. And sometimes, no matter how hard you try to avoid it, you occasionally get stung in the process.

10 · THE DELIGHTFUL HORROR OF FAMILY BIRDING

Everyone has a plan till they get punched in the mouth.

—Mike Tyson

Two decades ago, in the ardor of my twenties, I sought the sublime. The sublime I sought, in the most ordinary sense of the word, mirrored that of many freewheeling young adults stretching their wings for the first time. I was after lofty heights, majestic mountains, and large-scale inspiration. Now, in my fourth decade of life and as father of three young ones, sublime has been supplanted by another word: refuge. I crave it.

From the moment I awaken each morning, I am strafed by words and requests and noise. I am grateful for it and ultimately thankful, but like any parent, I seek breaks: short rest stops along the highway of life. Refuge, with all its connotations of retreat and tranquility, calls to me like the sublime used to. This is probably why I awoke at five a.m. last month to sneak out of my hotel room my family and I shared as we crossed the country. Gingerly, I eased the door shut, careful not to awaken the four sleeping bodies splayed across the beds like sardines. Minutes later I was out of Brigham City, Utah, and easing my dusty car along the gravel roads of the nearby Bear River Migratory Bird Refuge.

Bear River is a refuge like few others. With a concentrated

cauldron of the richest saline brew, the refuge offers a nutritious bounty with nearly every dive and dabble. Coupled with good vantage points and water nearly everywhere, it isn't surprising Terry Tempest Williams resonated with its ebb and flow as she did. So moved by Bear River, Williams penned Refuge, writing: "The birds and I share a natural history. It is a matter of rootedness, of living inside a place for so long that the mind and the imagination fuse." The city officials of Brigham City have taken a less poetic tack, boldly declaring their city the "Gateway to the World's Greatest Wild Bird Refuge" on a massive self-promotional sign that spans nearly six lanes of traffic.

My morning in Bear River easily lived up to its billing. Thousands of burgundy white-faced ibis mechanically marched across the berms and dikes. Black-necked stilts pirouetted across mudflats on impossibly thin, lipstick-colored legs. Grebes, pheasants, avocets, and then, rounding a bend, the ultimate *coup de grace* sedate along the roadside: a short-eared owl. I rolled down the window, cut the engine, and stared. Oversized eyes met mine in a timeless vigil. My gaze drifted over the bird, noting the feathered feet, loose barring down the breast, and facial discs so pronounced that the nearest kin could well have been orangutans. In the middle of the discs sat the school bus yellow eyes, ringed in so much black it was clear that makeup artists got carried away; this owl was the Jack Sparrow of the bird world, right off the set of Pirates of the Caribbean.

I wanted more time. But as usual with spontaneous owl encounters, the mysterious meter had expired. The owl tilted forward, pumped its wings powerfully, and flew off, its massive talons just missing the tops of the cattails as it melted into the morning haze. I exhaled, suddenly aware I hadn't breathed during the all-too-brief encounter. Despite the building heat, goose bumps ran down my spine. Smiling and satiated, I started the car and slowly left Bear River. I had found the refuge I'd sought. I'd also found a sliver of the sublime, not in the sense I used to seek, but more toward the word's etymology. "Sub" for "below," and "limen" for "threshold." In those piercing yellow eyes that reflected the intensity of my own, I'd found more than an owl; I'd found fearsome inspiration.

Back at the hotel, I tried to spread the wealth, recounting my Bear River experience for Linda and the kids. Ultimately I owed the entire experience to her. While I had focused on wiring the lights on our trailer and loading bikes before this cross-country trek, Linda had strategically chosen hotels near wildlife refuges. While sleep still ranked higher than birds in her hierarchy of goods, she knew how to keep me inspired.

Hotel staff clearing up the continental breakfast looked at me curiously as I dutifully listed the birds I'd seen for my numbers-obsessed son. For Indigo and Willow, I acted out the antics of a frantic rail that had briefly shared the road with me before hot-stepping into some rushes. After breakfast, I dragged all of them over to the impressive Bear River visitor center. We ogled exhibits, posed with avocet sculptures, and had snacks under a cacophony of nesting cliff swallows. Try as I might, however, I couldn't recreate the refuge I'd found.

Like other hardheaded, slow-learning dads, I tried again. A month later, after a few days cooped up in a new house in Oregon, Linda, her sister, and my three kids packed into the car for a short day excursion. I eagerly announced that we were headed to Tule Lake, a waterfowl magnet nestled on the southeastern flank of the Klamath Mountains just across the border in California. This was no mere lake, however. Like Bear River, it was a designated national wildlife refuge. Like so many other refuges had before, surely Tule Lake would deliver a needed dose of retreat and tranquility. Endless rafts of pelicans and grebes set off by the slanting rays of an evening sun played through my head. It would be picturesque for sure, perhaps with even a pinch of the sublime.

My intentions were flawless. Unfortunately, everything else was flawed. Initial zeal was extinguished before we'd even cleared the mountains near our home. The road, windier than a tangled extension cord, tied our stomachs into knots. "Slow down, Dad, you're killing me!" shouted Ezra woozily from the back. All I saw of Linda in the rearview mirror, squeezed into the back between Indigo and Willow, was her long brown hair that hung down to her feet like a curtain. Her head was buried deep in her hands. Backseats, nauseous kids, and twisty roads had precious little upside. I could read her thoughts: Tule Lake had better be good.

Our stomachs settled as we exchanged Oregon's mountains for its eastern plains. But just as quickly, we smacked into a wall of acrid smoke from one of the summer season's endless wildfires. We wheezed our way past a police officer, who, breathing into a mask, detoured us onto a side road. Our final turn, four miles from the lake, forced us onto freshly laid asphalt. The tar coated the car's undercarriage like recalcitrant phlegm. I slowed down to ease the asphalt assault. It was a slow crawl.

"Let's just find somewhere to pull over, sit down, and enjoy the snacks I've brought," Linda said, forcing an optimistic tone. "How about right out there!" She pointed to a wide turnout.

Eager to get out of the car and make something of this ill-fated trip, I pulled over. A long path led out to a well-built little building perched out on Tule Lake's north shore. A sign staked in the ground beside the beckoning path stated: "Wildlife Refuge Photography Bird Blind." "Perfect," Linda said. "We'll eat in the blind."

Halfway out, the wind picked up and all of the ducks that had been close lifted off and disappeared. Not one remained. By the time Indigo reached us at a run, every last coot and egret had also departed for quieter waters. Once in the blind, my short-lived optimism sank deeper than the last grebe. The blind, so welcoming and quaint on the outside, was the arachnid capital of the world. Cobwebs coated every bench and plank. This was a world wide web we'd rather not connect to.

Horrified, we backed out of the blind and spied a smaller one, resembling an outhouse, fifty yards off along another arm of the lake. Since the kids were the only ones who could fit inside, they took turns investigating the dilapidated structure. Two-year-old Willow was the last to enter. Fittingly, she was the one to discover the nest of wasps. "Ahhh!" Linda cried, yanking shell-shocked Willow out of the blind. Five wasps crawled on her hand. Whether in panic or pain, Willow took her cue and started howling hysterically.

This was defeat plain and simple. Time to raise the white flag. I grabbed the box of unopened snacks and sprinted for the car. My thought was simple and straightforward. Leave. Quickly. Like my family, I was tired, frustrated, hot, and hungry. Even worse, I felt stupid. What had I been thinking? Obviously I couldn't recreate inspired moments I'd had by myself. I needed refuge from this refuge.

While feelings of retreat and peace evaded us, we got at least halfway to sublime. In its older usage, sublime evokes a delightful horror, a fear followed by joy. It extends further than mere beauty, which inspires tenderness and affection without fear and trembling. Many a frustrated artist has been unable to capture this elusive quality. Irish writer and philosopher Edmund Burke perhaps described it best, writing that sublime moments inspired a sense of mind-filling terror, a healthy shock "that fills the mind with grand ideas and turns the soul in upon itself."

Thankfully, there was a decided lack of mind-filling terror on our return trip. We fortified ourselves at a grand buffet, navigated around the smoke and fires, and laughed about the delightful horror of the Tule Lake bird blinds. As I switched on my high beams to better navigate the winding roads on our way back through the mountains, my sister-in-law uttered a word that again sent goose bumps down my spine. "Owl!" she gasped, pointing to a striking silhouette atop a large Douglas fir. I pulled over, positioning the car to give us all a vantage point. A deep indigo sky outlined the owl's barrel form, accentuating the ear tufts. Its head swiveled robotically, right then left. The body tilted slightly forward, and the owl lifted off, dissolving into the inky night.

Beautiful, sublime, or maybe just cool—I have no idea what the rest of my family thought as we watched the owl. Nor what they thought of our entire harebrained excursion to Tule Lake. I do know we managed to capture something that many don't, something momentary and elusive. Our moment with the owl offered a collective retreat—a temporary speechless tranquility—from life's daily onslaught of words, noise, and mindless distraction. Tule Lake never claimed to be the world's greatest refuge. But it gave us delightful horror. And as a father of three in my fourth decade of life, I'll take any refuge I can get.

Part II

THE SKY IS OUR CLASSROOM

Juniper titmouse

11 · THE GRAND TITMOUSE

So, naturalists observe, a flea
Has smaller fleas that on him prey;
And these have smaller still to bite 'em
And so proceed ad infinitum.

—Jonathan Swift

"You mean, you're going to take your students to Arizona but you're not going to visit the Grand Canyon?!" my colleague exclaimed incredulously, tipping back in his office chair.

"It's a bird class," I replied, standing in the doorframe. "Not a geology class."

"Well, I'd rethink that if I were you." He handed me an Arizona guidebook. "You can't bring students to Arizona and deprive them of the Grand Canyon. They'll never forgive you."

"What they don't see won't kill them." I stuffed the guidebook in my leather bag and spun on my heels to head to my next class.

Six months later, I stood at the Grand Canyon's Mather Point, surrounded by eighteen wide-eyed college students, many of whom were witnessing the canyon for the first time. The sun had just crested the canyon wall, sending deep blue, slanting shadows westward. Not yet set aflame by the sun, the red canyon walls showed subtle shades of lavender and peach. Each breath we exhaled enshrouded us like gossamer. And setting off the scene spectacularly was a dark bird angling toward us.

The bird, a zone-tailed hawk, conformed to the canyon's irregular crags and spires, passing just under our lookout as it scanned for sun-hungry lizards. After three weeks of straining our necks looking skyward, here we watched comfortably from above. No aching neck. No glare. No worries about roasting our retinas. We fell silent; not out of fatigue, but out of awe. This was a peerless moment, one that lasts while so many others pass away. While Arizona had birdier spots, the Grand Canyon had perks all its own. Watching raptors as God does—and maybe with a smidgeon of God's appreciation—was certainly one of them.

As the hawk slowly turned into a speck, I addressed the group. "Let's continue to amble along the rim and see what else soars below us."

We pulled ourselves away from the breathtaking viewpoint and headed back to the rim trail. As we did so, the first of an endless stream of tour buses arrived and scores of camera-wielding people engulfed us. Through the rising tide of bodies, I spied a titmouse in a juniper tree not much taller than myself.

"Titmouse, twelve o'clock!" I yelled, oblivious to the jostling crowd. By now, my students well understood my enthusiastic directives, and they quickly gathered round. But the fresh-off-the-bus tourists were befuddled. Many had flown halfway around the world for a glimpse of the Grand Canyon. Now within a short walk of one of the canyon's most iconic viewpoints, they most certainly did not expect to encounter people staring in the wrong direction! And at an uninspiring Charlie Brown tree, no less. Unable to help themselves, many tourists, bedecked in large-pocketed vests and oversized hats, clustered around us. Surely something grand must be in this tree.

Just then, one of my students fought through the crowd. "Eli, there's another raptor soaring through the canyon!"

Caught up in the moment, I retorted with words that haunted me the rest of the trip. Words I'd like to blame on the strong coffee I'd guzzled and the crisp canyon air. They were words I meant—and only now, upon reflection—fully understand.

"Ignore the canyon! We've got a juniper titmouse!"

A small man holding a brochure in one hand and a cola in the other seized the moment. Up on his toes, he leaned in jowl-to-jowl with me, trying to find the source of my excitement.

"What are you looking at?" he asked. He took a swig of his soda but kept staring at the tree, tilting his head slightly.

"The bird teed up on that twig." I pointed straight at the titmouse. "Follow the end of my finger!"

"I don't see! I don't see!" He sounded almost panicked. Another wave of tourists pressed in. All of them—at least sixty people from faraway countries—were ignoring the Grand Canyon and craning their necks at a small tree. Because of me. Within seconds of seeing the seventh wonder of the world, they were all held up for a small, gray, nondescript bird. A bird they would never hear of, nor ever see in documentaries, IMAX films, brochures, or coffee-table books. A bird that, outside of a small circle of birders and ornithologists, nobody will ever care about.

This particular homely titmouse, likely flabbergasted by its unexpected stardom, nervously vacated its perch in the juniper and disappeared into the canyon's forest.

The short man took another long swig and addressed me again. "I still don't see it."

"It just flew off," I replied sheepishly.

"Was it a special bird?" he asked, exasperated.

"Very special," I mumbled. But a wave of long-sequestered self-consciousness washed over me and I simply couldn't endure any more questioning. An inexplicable chasm had opened between the soda-swigging man and me. Like the hawk and the titmouse, it seemed we were different species. "Let's go, gang!" I shouted, anxious to disappear as the titmouse had.

Away from the busloads, tranquility returned. But as our blood pressures lowered, our temperatures rose. While the night had been frosty, the sun had reclaimed the sky and was now intent on roasting everything below it, including us. We stripped off layers and pulled out sunglasses. What was amazing, it occurred to me, was that so many creatures here dealt with such vicissitudes daily.

While the juniper titmouse lacked breathtaking intricacy on the outside, it housed a canyon of wonders on the inside. One of the greatest of these was a Lilliputian metabolic engine that derived enough energy from juniper seeds to maintain its twenty-five-gram body at 112 degrees. Each night, the titmouse huddled in a cavity, at the mercy of fickle temperatures. We had our own wondrous metabolic engines, of course, but we needed fancy sleeping bags, multiple layers, and a warm van to survive the night.

As for layers, the titmouse had only its feathers. But oh, what feathers! In addition to allowing flight, these multifunctional miracles are indispensable for trapping air and surviving frigid nights, thanks to an intricate structure.

The lower portion, the part we grab when we find a feather under the feeder, is the calamus. It's the calamus, or quill, that was used to write the Magna Carta and Declaration of Independence. The calamus is both flexible and hollow, giving needed lightness for flight. While the calamus is critical, the vane is the real wonder. It's the part we can't resist running our fingers along. When we do this against the grain, we unlock the barbs, possibly unzipping smaller barbules and maybe even unhooking still smaller barbicels. If we go with the grain, we rehook, rezip, and relock. For us, it's playing with nature's Velcro. For a bird, it's preening, and necessary for surviving sub-zero nights on the Grand Canyon's rim. Below the contour feathers—the outermost feathers we see—the juniper titmouse uses its 8,500 varied feathers to trap a fraction of an inch of air to support its metabolic engine.

The juniper titmouse nestled in a ponderosa pine cavity faces a routine yet formidable foe each night. As the temperature dips, it raises its feathers and fluffs out, fortifying its insulation. At the same time, blood circulation is slowed to its extremities as the bird burns the precious fuel it stored the day before. If it dies in the night, it's not a feather malfunction; it's due to poor foraging. But equipped with its intricate array of feathers, made from the insoluble protein keratin, the titmouse is well-adapted to survive the night and watch the sun rise over the canyon as we had.

While I was steeped in feather wonder, my students were not. So it wasn't a surprise when one of my snarkier students seized a lull and remarked, "Hey everybody, ignore the Grand Canyon and look at this little gray bird!" Everybody laughed.

Sheepish and still too close to the moment, I was unable to dig out an equally snarky retort. My ill-conceived directive was now cemented; I was the butt of this joke, and remained so for the rest of the trip.

My Arizona adventure ended, and spring turned into late summer. As with all my trips, detailed memories soon faded into snapshots and selective sound bites, surfacing only when triggered. Two months later, for example, I noticed another titmouse—this time a tufted titmouse—while relaxing on my parents' porch at their lake cottage in the endless mountain region of Pennsylvania. Apart from the slight brown wash on its flanks, it was almost a spitting image of the juniper titmouse I'd seen in Arizona. Small, gray, and drab. For most people, just part of the scenery.

True to form, I ignored the beautiful lake and focused solely on the titmouse. It bounced along the branch, cocking its crested head left and right. And then it happened: a memorable moment borne only of focused attention. Out of nowhere, the titmouse was strafed by a small, feathered missile. So small was the attacker that I assumed it was an insect. But the assailant instantly returned, and I caught an iridescent shimmer. A female ruby-throated hummingbird. She buzzed the dumbstruck titmouse time and again.

Unnerved by such spiteful determination, the titmouse flew off. Not long after, the hummingbird melted into the hemlock branch. I traced the branch's contours and soon found a little mossy bump not far from where the titmouse had landed: a nest, virtually invisible unless you had watched the bird settle upon it, as I had. Soon another bird—a white-breasted nuthatch—landed on the hemlock's trunk, head characteristically cocked up as if held by a neck brace. The nuthatch landed on the limb, just feet from the incubating hummingbird. The hummingbird utterly ignored it. Likewise over the next half-hour, the hummingbird ignored a downy woodpecker, black-capped chickadee, and red-eyed vireo. When the titmouse returned, the hummingbird gave chase yet again.

This little hummingbird, it dawned on me, was birding! It was identifying specific species and harassing or ignoring them accordingly. Unlike many of its innocuous neighbors, the titmouse must have a taste for eggs, scrambled or otherwise. Like me, the hummingbird was focused on details overlooked by most.

Caught up in the drama in the trees, I hardly noticed when Indigo, four-years-old at the time, dragged an oversized stuffed panda out onto the porch and placed it at my feet. My daughter has always loved pandas. She cannot sleep without one, and I am partly responsible for her collection of well over a dozen. I like her panda affection. What isn't to like in a black-and-white bear that eats vegetables? Sure, the world is chock-full of panda lovers, and the cuddly bear hogs lots of conservation attention. But judging from the extreme habitat loss pandas have endured, they obviously need even more. The same is true for most of the charismatic megafauna we share our planet with.

At the same time, I'm wondering if we've mixed up our priorities. Perhaps we're too preoccupied by life's grandest things, like canyons and pandas. Perhaps this is what has led us into our current predicament. Maybe if we disproportionately liked the little things, or even noticed the little things, we wouldn't be in the extinction crisis we're in. In her Pulitzer Prize-winning book, *The Sixth Extinction*, Elizabeth Kolbert claims that the difference between the current mass extinction event and the five that preceded it is that this one is clearly human-caused. Not only are humans the cause, we may also be the victims. As Paul Ehrlich stated: "In pushing other species to extinction, humanity is busy sawing off the limb on which it perches." I share Ehrlich's concern. And at the very least, I contend that if we learned to see titmice for what they really are—vast canyons of complexity—conserving larger creatures like pandas would come a lot more naturally.

I picked up Indigo's panda, which enticed her to crawl up into my lap. While she sucked her thumb contentedly, I thought back to my day at the Grand Canyon.

In stark contrast to the busloads of tourists who snapped selfies, bought a few trinkets, and soon left, my students couldn't get enough. Yes, the canyon held them spellbound. But they were after the canyon's actors, too, from the stars down to the supporting cast.

The reason for this has always been right in front of me. It's so simple and nondescript, like the juniper titmouse, that I've overlooked it for decades. To truly appreciate life's grandest wonders, sometimes you have to ignore the canyon.

Chuck-will's widow

12 · ABSURD BIRD WORDS

When ideas fail, words come in very handy.

—Johann Wolfgang von Goethe

"Let's go get those goatsuckers!" I said to my gaggle of five ornithology students. Three of them stood up and grabbed their gear, ready for action. But two of them looked at me with wrinkled brows.

"Goatsuckers?" Adam asked.

"Yeah, you know, that chuck-will's-widow we heard. Let's go find it." I smiled as nonchalantly as I could. My explanation was intentionally vague. I'd give them a longer, more fulfilling etymology during a later, slower part of the bird walk. Now, however, was time for the chase.

Most of us can remember our exhilarating moments on a bird walk. The times when the heron stabs a fish, the eagle soars overhead, and the loon leers with ruby-red eyes. Such walks are punctuated with unbridled enthusiasm. Hermit thrush, three o'clock! Peregrine stooping overhead! Do you hear that bittern? It's in the reeds right in front of us!

Our binoculars bounce, our cameras click, and our field guides flutter like warbler wings. In such times, the sights and sounds are too many and our senses happily succumb to the endless stimuli. These are the wonderful walks you remember. For a trip leader, like myself, such walks are downright intoxicating.

But we also know too well that nature moves in fits and spurts. What is here today is gone tomorrow. And a lot of the time, seeing something great is simply being in the right place at the right time. Even during the wee morning hours in a wetland, when everything should be everywhere, stillness and silence may blanket the swamp. For a leader, such moments may be tediously torturous, akin to watching a pot boil. You feel guilty and responsible. Your participants want to experience nature—lots of species and lots of interactions—so much that their expectant eyes are boring holes into the back of your head. It's your fault that the day doesn't resemble a National Geographic documentary.

Really good leaders don't feel this. Why? They are masters of diversion. They redirect the group's attention to nature you can count on: trees, flowers, rocks, or even pinecones for that matter. They bend down and behold, look at this odd, upright pinecone! Closer inspection reveals that the pinecone is no pinecone at all; it's cancer-root. The savvy leader points out that common names are often misleading, as there is no scientific evidence suggesting the cone-shaped, cream-colored plant either prevents or causes cancer. The name may have come from its tendency to form galls—"tumors"—on oak roots. Instead of sending up leaves to collect chlorophyll like a well-behaved plant, cancer-root sends roots down searching out oak roots to tap into and suck nutrients from. Cancer-root is a pirate, looting other plants of their bounty.

A better name, the leader suggests, is bear corn. Not only does the inflorescence resemble a corncob but bears also crave it when they emerge from hibernation. Why? Because bear corn has laxative properties, allowing them to purge their plumbing. If I went half a year without a movement, I'd binge on bear corn too.

The *coup de grace* occurs, of course, when the non-photosynthesizing, parasitic plant is passed around for consumption. Bear corn is an excellent source of nourishment, high in beta-carotene, potassium, magnesium, and vitamin C. But it's bitter as sin, in other words, perfect for passing around to unsuspecting—and by now heavily distracted—birders. Aficionados claim bear corn is heavenly when sautéed in butter and garnished with bacon. Yeah, and so are old socks. I need to be either shriveled up on a desert island or chronically constipated before I snack on this survival food.

Few of us carry around such encyclopedic trivia about obscure plants. And most of us aren't emerging mycologists or genius geologists. We don't know what a basidiocarp is, nor do we know if the aster underfoot is growing on granite or garnet. Yes, we aspire to be renaissance naturalists. But we're about two thousand species behind. So what do we do? Is all lost? Should we give up leading? Absolutely not.

All we have to do is rekindle the colloquial and resuscitate the obscure. Obsolete? Great! Old-fashioned? Even better! Shouting butter-butt (yellow-rumped warbler) on a slow July bird walk is akin to shouting fire in a crowded theater. The same goes for log-cocks (pileated woodpeckers) and thunder-pumpers (bitterns). A well seen white-breasted nuthatch wows a beginning birder. But for students halfway through an ornithology course, it's just another white-breasted nuthatch. As a group leader, do you point out the nuthatch and trudge along? No! You stop the group, point to the bird, and shout, "Devil downhead!" If that doesn't snap the collective stupor, you wax about the wonders of this abundant and bipedal "tree mouse."

These weird names, and not the more useful current taxonomy, stick in my skull like chewing gum on my shoe. Is it trivial? Yes. Is it useful? Not really. So why use it? Because, it holds an audience's interest. And without an active audience, your winsome walk through the woods becomes a forced march.

The chuck-will's-widow we had heard from our campfire was now leading us along a wild goose chase. Or a wild goatsucker chase, that is. We still hadn't even glimpsed our quarry. Every time it called, we followed. Every time we drew near, the widow vanished into the inky Missouri night like a feathered phantom. One thing was obvious. My group's spirits were fading fast. "Let's make one more stab," I told my weary followers. Stoically, they consented. I needed a diversion. Quickly. "So why do you think they call 'em goatsuckers?" I asked.

"Because they're vampire birds?" a flannel-shirted guy, Ethan, ventured.

"You're close," I said. "Obviously these birds are hard to find. They're usually seen at dusk and dawn and on bright moonlit nights, making them mysterious to most. Their mouths open wide. Just wide enough to fit . . ." I paused for effect, making sure I had everyone's attention. I did. "Well, they fit perfectly on the teat of a goat. Hypothetically, of course . . ."

"No way!" said Brianna, inadvertently shining her head-lamp straight into my eyes.

"Way!" I retorted, momentarily blinded in the midst of my feeble attempt to speak student lingo. "A while back, some people thought they flew into barns at dusk, gorged on goat milk all night, and then flew out in the morning before the farmer awoke."

"Not true!" several students said in unison.

"Right," I countered. "It's a myth. 'Insect sucker' would be a more appropriate name. That's what these gifted fliers actually eat."

Just then the chuck-will's-widow called loudly from a co-nifer grove. "Let's go single file," I whispered. We crept into the grove, our flashlight beams slicing arcs in the branches like lightsabers. This time the widow kept calling. Slowly but surely, we were zeroing in. The sound steadily amplified until it shook our bones. Shoulder to shoulder, we scanned and scanned.

"There it is!" Brianna exclaimed in an excited whisper. All our lights joined as one and illuminated a beautiful chuck-will's-widow perched upright on a limb calling with all of his amorous might. The bird was so close we could have smoothed his ruffled feathers with a long pole.

"Now that is gorgeous goatsucker!" I exclaimed after a long pause. The obscure term, unknown an hour ago, was now understood—and appreciated—by all. After a few minutes, slowly and silently, we filed out of the woods and onto a paved road. Whispers gave way to lively conversation. We had seen something special. Now was the time for reveling in its mystery.

Inevitably, however, our chuck-will's-widow high wore off and the only sounds were those of our sneakers on the pavement. The time was ripe again to rekindle the colloquial.

"Next year, we're going to Maine," I stated matter-of-factly.

"What's to see there?" Ethan asked.

"What's not to see in Maine?" I retorted. "But I think we'll start with hell-divers, timberdoodles, and skunk heads."

Silence. Although I couldn't confirm it in the darkness, I knew some of my students were smiling and others were raising a bemused eyebrow. They were onto me. I didn't need a response—only a heightened sense of wonder. The recipe for bettering a boring bird walk is pretty straightforward. Start with a bird or two. Then add a pinch of colloquial yeast and stir lightly. Boredom will soon dissipate. And in its stead, wonder will rise.

Lucy's warbler

13 · SOLE RECIPIENTS OF GRACE

For me, every hour is grace.

—Elie Wiesel

"Reverse sex polyandry!" I yell. My students stare at me blankly. "Right there, that bird—the jacana—practices reverse sex polyandry!"

Having hollered this out several times on several continents now, I've come to realize it's a concept I'm perhaps a little too infatuated with. And like other overly passionate professors, I want my students to understand my fascination. Fortunately, right now, in a boat in Costa Rica, one does. Greg.

"What is reverse sex poly . . . poly . . . ?"

"Andry!" I finish for him, eager to prey upon his curiosity. "It's one of those cool exceptions in mating systems where the male sits on the eggs while the female flies the coop. Less than one percent of bird species practice it," I add, hoping to drive home the ethological spectacle foraging right alongside us on some floating vegetation.

Ever since first reading about reverse sex polyandry, I've devoured everything I could dig up on the subject. Some of my intrigue is purely academic, as I have puzzled how natural selection could select for such a unique lifestyle. But most of my intrigue, truth be told, is rooted in my own relationship with my selfless wife, Linda.

Not because of the multiple matings, mind you, but more

by the fact that reverse sex polyandry is accompanied by a reversal of sexual roles in which males perform all, or at least the lion's share, of the parental duties (incidentally, other than defending territories and occasionally assisting in toppling a buffalo, male lions practice precious little cub rearing, or anything, for that matter). A generation ago, I doubt my intrigue would have passed first base. Cultural mores of that era were such that husbands and fathers may have eaten dinner and slept in the home but spent most of their time out of it, at work. This was my dad's generation. And even more so my grandfather's. Perhaps unsurprisingly, those norms ebbed as more and more women sought careers. Two-income families became commonplace. For those of my generation who have figured out how to live on one income, I have an ever-growing number of male friends who have decided to remain at home with the kids while their wives bring home the bacon. In other words, many of my peers have followed in the long-toed footsteps of the northern jacana.

But I haven't. My wife and I have a throwback relationship where I'm the breadwinner and she's the bread maker. At least for now, we're the ninety-nine percent of other birds. Although I marvel at the jacana, I haven't yet followed its intrepid lead. Undeniably, raising the brood is the highest good. And it's also ridiculously difficult to do well. My wife sacrifices sleep, acclaim, and breathing space on a daily basis. Ask any young mother who gets a chance to work outside the home—even part-time—and they often relish the opportunity to go to work. Logging time in the office, no matter how mundane or stressful, is at the very least getting released from a cage with a ten-pound tyrant, or a collection of them.

And that's exactly it: when the cacophony becomes too ear splitting, I can get in my truck and drive to work. Even though my truck has a dilapidated muffler and an assortment of rattles, it offers me deafening quiet. I'm so busy savoring solitude that I become the annoying guy who drives well under the speed limit. It's my thought time, my quiescence; it affords me the luxury to think about things besides diapers and dishcloths. Things like reverse sex polyandry.

I certainly haven't thought about it like some, however. Just the other day, I struck up conversation with a serious-looking German while exiting Ruaha National Park in Tanzania. "See anything special?" I asked, expecting him to rattle off lions or leopards like a typical tourist.

"No." He frowned at a map in front of him. "I was looking for black coucals." Black coucals?! What? Who comes to one of the world's best national parks and looks for one of East Africa's blandest birds? This guy was no tourist. I turned to face him.

"Does it parasitize other birds?" I asked, my curiosity exploding.

"No," he replied tersely. "But," he added, "it's the only altricial bird in the world that practices reverse sex polyandry. Did you happen to see any? I'm looking for a new study site." Fortunately, I was just nerdy enough to indeed know where I'd seen black coucals and relayed the info.

Satisfied, the German fished out a business card and handed it to me. "I'm with the Max Planck Institute of Ornithology. Wolfgang," he said, extending his hand.

"Eli," I replied. "So tell me, how does polyandry evolve in altricial birds?"

"That is *the* question!" He broke into a large smile. "I have been studying this question for ten years!"

Next to Wolfgang, I was a lightweight. But it was somehow comforting to see that some ornithological questions are so tangled that even after ten years of devoted study, the answers remain obscure. Scientists have pretty much sorted out how reverse sex polyandry has arisen in the few cases it has. In birds like the jacana and some sandpipers, the females can lay more clutches during a breeding season when they leave the incubating and raising duties to the male. So it's not like the females are laying eggs and then vacationing on the beach in Mombasa. Once a clutch is laid, they form another harem of males, choose one, and lay another clutch.

A male left with a clutch, meanwhile, needs to incubate the eggs for a little less than a month once his one-night stand has ended. Tedious, yes. But not terrible. Male jacanas are savvy; they rely on solar. On hot, steamy days, males only need to incubate a clutch for seven percent of the day on a nest laid on floating vegetation. The sun does the rest. Cool, cloudy days are more difficult, requiring the male to sit for seventy percent of his day. While the sun keeps the eggs warm, the male can go gallivanting, feeding himself and scoping out other females frolicking about the swamp.

The male has another card up his sleeve too. The young are precocial. Able to feed themselves soon after birth, the male doesn't have the onerous duties that come with helpless babies otherwise known as altricial young, in biology lingo. No night feedings, no diapers, no trapped burps. This doesn't mean the male sits on the couch with a six-pack watching reruns of Seinfeld. He's attentive to the many dangers that abound in a swamp, be they monitor lizards, snakes, or otters. With the help of a modified radius bone—bow-shaped and flattened— the doting father literally picks up his young underneath his wings and escorts them to safety. He can carry all four if he has to. This system works well for the jacana and its precocial young. For the altricial young of the black coucal—Wolfgang's bird—it's a conundrum indeed.

Reverse sex polyandry was so unknown two hundred years ago that it even confused the great John James Audubon, who mislabeled the males and females in his phalarope plates. It turns out that sexual size dimorphism—when the sexes are visibly distinct—is also reversed, causing the females to loom larger and appear more colorful than the males. They're not just larger; they're nearly twice the size, rendering males entirely subordinate. I love that fact. Just as I love other historical accounts of women in the vanguard. History shows us how the deck of discrimination has been stacked unevenly. So I'm doubly inspired by the women, who often by sheer will alone have found ways to wiggle out of this historical yoke and lift off.

Mimicking the dazzling male warblers that command our attention each spring, men have long done so in advancing the field of ornithology. Countless organizations bear their names. Entities like the National Audubon Society, the Wilson Ornithological Society, and the Roger Tory Peterson Institute, not to mention well over two thousand species of birds. Wilson's warbler, Townsend's warbler, MacGillivray's warbler; the list goes on. But just as some birders don't take time to identify female fall warblers, many haven't taken the time to recognize the great women who pushed the frontiers of ornithology. These women have received passing—if any—acclaim for their endeavors. My squadron of female bird heroes is legion, however, from the likes of the writer Florence Merriam Bailey to the insightful Mabel Osgood Wright and the far-sighted conservationist Rosalie Edge. Through a combination of creativity, steadfastness, and sheer will, these juggernauts influenced many and saw the value in birds and conservation when most did not.

John James Audubon deservedly gets lots of credit for jumpstarting bird interest in North America. But his wife, Lucy, as with many women of that era, played a pivotal role as well. Upon John James's death in 1851, Lucy took up teaching to make ends meet. One of her pupils, aptly named George Bird Grinnell, was as precocious as a newly hatched jacana. He became enamored with his highly intelligent and tenderhearted teacher. Their relationship blossomed to a point where Lucy became "Grandma Audubon" to George. As a token of her fondness, Lucy bequeathed to him an arresting painting of a golden eagle attacking a lamb that had hung in her house for years. The painting was symbolic. When the tutorial had ended, Lucy had skillfully sunk ornithology's talons deep into George. It changed him forever. He enjoyed a distinguished career as an ornithologist and conservationist, eventually founding the Audubon Society. By the time of his death in 1938, Grinnell was heralded by the *New York Times* as "the father of American conservation." All of these accomplishments, arguably, can be traced to Lucy's timely influence.

While I laud Lucy, I am perhaps most taken by a woman about whom I know almost nothing: Grace Darling Coues. While Grace's direct contribution to ornithology is unknown, it was obvious she supported and inspired her restless brother, Elliott Coues. I base this on a single sentence Elliott wrote about his eighteen-year-old sister after he discovered a new warbler in the Rocky Mountains in 1864. "My affection and respect," Elliott penned, "keep pace with my appreciation of her true loveliness of character." As was the custom of nineteenth-century naturalists, Elliott Coues wanted to name the exquisite warbler to honor another person he valued. Rather than honor yet another male mentor or friend, Elliott wanted the esteem to go to Grace, whom he adored. Elliott's request was granted by Spencer Fullerton Baird and in 1865, the little white and yellow warbler that flits about the highest-most branches in Arizona's pine forests became Grace's warbler, a name it carries to this day.

For the record, Grace's warbler doesn't practice reverse sex polyandry. Paralleling my own spousal relationship, the female does the heavy lifting while the male spastically flits about the canopy performing the usual warbler song and dance. I was performing my own annual song and dance last May in Arizona for my annual ornithology class. Linda, meanwhile, was at home tending our nest of three fledglings all under age ten. My life, in other words, had a twinge of fun and adventure while Linda was back in the mind-numbing trenches of diapers and trapped burps.

The course had been an easy sell. Since most every student hailed from the Northeast, Arizona offered an intriguing taste of the exotic. Human-shaped cacti, radical rock formations, and, of course, the requisite stop at the grandest wonder of all, the Grand Canyon (not to mention the grand titmouse, of course). We were after raptors, roadrunners, and, most of all, a glimpse of the long-imperiled California condor, which we opted to dedicate an entire day to seeking.

One of our first finds was Lucy's warbler, a cute gray warbler of the desert. While I wished the bird had been named in honor of Lucy Audubon, it was for Lucy Hunter Baird, daughter of the aforementioned Spencer Baird, who served as the secretary of the Smithsonian Institution. Either way, the warbler honored a woman and I was happy with that. Also, it was far easier to remember than the confusing warbler names of the east, like black-throated green warbler and black-throated blue warbler. We went from one wonder to the next, pyrrhuloxias to petroglyphs, until, on the final day of our trip, we arrived at the Grand Canyon. As a class, we meandered the south rim, scrutinizing every passing raven and raptor. After three hours in the sun, my students started wilting. The time had come to redeploy. "We'll meet again at five o'clock," I instructed. "The rest of the day is yours to bird, rest, or enjoy the canyon however you wish."

Having logged every hour together for the past week, the students were anxious for some solo time. By the time I emerged from a nearby restroom, everybody had evaporated.

I was alone. Having failed to see wild condors years ago in California despite many attempts, I was not about to give up this golden opportunity and squander my time in a gift shop. I would seek some shade. But my eyes would stay glued to the skies above the south rim.

The hours passed far too quickly. Nestled under a copse of piñon pine, I relished a boisterous couple of rock wrens, ogled a western tanager that hung in an oak like an ornament, and squandered a happy hour stymied by the song of a black-headed grosbeak that sounded far too much like a robin. Despite my unceasing attention, no condor soared past my perch.

Naturally I was a little late arriving to our five o'clock meeting. Excited faces revealed I'd missed something special. Emily and Katrina wasted no time in telling me what I'd missed. "Eli, we saw condors!"

"Where?" I demanded. "Take me!"

"They're gone!"

"When?"

"It was an hour ago, during the ranger program. Right in the middle of the condor rehabilitation talk, two flew past! Our ranger lady stopped everything to point them out!"

"Did anybody else in our class see them?" I implored jealously.

"Nope. Just us!" Emily said. Although both students had generous spirits, I could tell they were savoring the special delight that comes from being sole recipients of grace.

"You two don't know how lucky you are! As for the rest of us," I said, tapping my watch, "let's all be back at the vans in a half hour to get back to camp!"

Everybody scattered to restrooms and gift shops. I remained seated at a picnic table. Reading my mixed emotions like a book, my perceptive teacher's assistant, Lisa, sat down next to me. "Have you ever seen a Virginia's warbler?" she asked.

"Uh, no."

"Well I know where one is. At least it was there a few minutes ago."

"Let's go!" I said, my spirit rebounding.

"Follow me." We beelined back to the rim. Within minutes, we had found Lisa's Virginia's warbler. It was as skittish as a gnatcatcher and looked like one too, except for a splash of yellow on its breast and vent and a small, chestnut yarmulke. But what struck me most was its name. This bird wasn't named after the state of Virginia. It's a western bird. Rather, it was yet another bird named after a woman, this time the wife of William W. Anderson, a US Army surgeon who first recorded the bird in 1858.

"How'd you find this great bird?" I asked.

"Not sure, maybe we heard it first," Lisa replied nonchalantly.

First, my female students were finding condors. Now they were leading me to warblers I'd never seen. Here on this trip to Arizona, while Linda was dutifully tending the nest in New York, women were leading the way. I was grateful. It pleased me that other men like Elliott Coues and William Anderson, generations before mine, had shared similar gratitude for the women in their lives.

The next morning I crawled out of my tent. I felt Lilliputian under the stand of towering ponderosa pines. I yawned and stretched. As I reached skyward, an unfamiliar trill filtered down from the limbs overhead. Was it a junco? No. This was different. I made some "spishing" sounds to arouse the bird's curiosity. It worked. An overtly inquisitive warbler flew down from the canopy and bounced along a low branch, turning its head to and fro as it inspected my blowsy bedhead and mismatched outfit.

This, I knew, was none other than Grace's warbler, a bird I'd only enjoyed in the pages of my bird books. It was the warbler named for Grace Darling Coues, whom her brother wrote of having "true loveliness of character." It was an ethereal moment, my breath condensing in dissipating clouds while the warbler preened in a small patch of slanting sunlight. This was a bird I'd remember more than any raptor or roadrunner. Not for its special appearance or song. But rather for its simple yet weighty name: Grace. This is what Linda had granted me since the day we got married. It's what she grants me today. It's a special gift because our young, like those of songbirds, are altricial. We have an odd partnership. Yes, we argue and fight like most couples. But it has evolved through its particular hurdles in its own unique way. Even though it's odd—like the systems of the black coucal and the northern jacana—it works.

Knowing me, people often ask Linda if she, too, likes birds. Her reply is always the same. "I like birds," she quips, "but somebody has to mind the nest." Most people smile and are satisfied by her tongue-in-cheek answer. But I'm not. It conceals far too much. I know that Linda would love to stroll along the Grand Canyon and wake up in a primeval forest. But like ninety-nine percent of the birds in the world, she faithfully remains at the nest. Not because it's fair or just, but rather (like so many women before her) because she has a true loveliness of character. And because of this, she overflows with grace.

14 · Film Fallout

The enthusiasm of naturalists is very apt to surprise ordinary people.

—William Swainson

I'm a slightly nefarious ornithology professor. Obviously, I want my students to learn. Even more, I want them to become like me. No, I don't want them to wear mismatched outfits and tell jokes that do little more than raise eyebrows. Rather, I want them to become birders. Desperately. We all want people to enjoy what we enjoy to some degree; I'm just more determined than most. I want my students to watch, chase, study, and stalk birds—not only for the duration of the course, but also for the rest of their lives. An interest in birds, I'm betting, begets an interest in the natural world, a first crucial step toward conservation.

I mitigate my mischievous intent by being open about it. "What's the purpose of an apple tree?" I routinely ask my perplexed students on the first day of class. Inevitably, one overeager student falls into my trap.

"To produce apples!"

"No! To produce more apple *trees*!" I exclaim, raising my arms to the sky. I've set this trap so many times that my next movements are automatic. I find a vacant desk, perch myself upon it, and measure out my words. "Now . . . what's the purpose of a birder?"

It's a rhetorical question, of course, and I gleefully stare out at the blank expressions. One by one, I watch them smile. Eye rolling follows. But that doesn't bother me. Point made.

Selfishly intentioned as I am, I don't judge my success by the number of students that ace the final exam. Rather, I judge them by their journals, in which everyone is instructed to write down field notes, concepts, and the feelings they have about the birds we see. I tell them that the feelings part is more for them than for me, to work out their ornithological angst. Really the reverse is true. The journals are for me. By reading them, I determine how successful my attempts have been in making the sky their classroom. The journals tell me how birdbrained they've become.

As expected, I get the whole spectrum. Some think birding is pure silliness. Other chair-fillers are apathetic, in it for the credits alone. And then those coveted few—the ones that love and cherish every moment spent tromping through a mosquito-infested swamp. These few I know will keep their binoculars around their necks the rest of their lives. Such enthusiastic ones keep me ticking and keep me teaching. But they're not the best. Even better is the once-a-course student who begins thinking birding is silly but ends up like me—passionate. A rarity, indeed. Such a student joins my treasured flock, a subset of disciples I attempt to nurture well after the course ends.

This year something new and deeply troubling happened. Something I couldn't blow off. One of my zealous students, Liana, who started the course strongly, slowly ebbed in enthusiasm. At first, she loved every field trip, every bird, and every topic—be it molting or migration. As time progressed, I watched her grow despondent, apathetic even. She remained attentive and polite. But her fire was gone. Fearful that I was the sole cause and wanting to keep intact my fragile ego, I did my best to ignore it. Soon enough, the course was over and I still had no answer for her disheartening journey. As the students filed out of the room, they handed in their journals. I forced a smile as Liana walked up.

Oddly, she returned a warm and enthusiastic smile as she handed me a leather-bound notebook. I stared at her, utterly confused. Her smile remained. Nor was it the superficial one she'd worn the last few weeks. This was real. Liana was back. "Can I have this back really soon?" she asked eagerly. "I'm going to need it over the summer."

"Sure," I said. "But I thought . . ." My mumbled sentence trailed off. It didn't matter. Liana spun on her heels and waltzed out the door.

I took the pile of journals back to my office and started with Liana's. It didn't take me long to unravel the mystery. One of her reflective entries, at the midpoint of the course, said it all:

I find myself growing more and more attuned with the natural world around me. And I really enjoy finding birds . . . But the film we watched today changed all that. I don't want to be like any of them. I don't want to be obsessed. I don't want to become any of those people.

I paused, laid the journal on my desk, and sat back in my chair. Now things were coming together. The film Liana referred to was *The Big Year*, based on a book by Mark Obmascik. The book and film are based on a true story that describes the incredible competition that three obsessed birders took part in to see the most birds possible in a calendar year.

The demanding nature of my ornithology course, riddled as it is with six-hour labs, had led me to show The Big Year. It was a well-deserved break—like a warbler touching down to refuel during migration. Everybody had seemed to enjoy it at the time. But for Liana, The Big Year had some big effects. And although I knew the film would have some fallout, I certainly hadn't expected this much.

Fallout plays a role in *The Big Year*, too. To build their respective lists, the three birders travelled to Texas to take advantage of a storm front that forced hundreds of thousands of spring migrants to the ground. Ask any travel agent; a suddenly changed itinerary isn't too unusual. Weather can be fickle. Most birds patiently wait for ideal conditions. For northbound migrations, clear skies and slight southerly tailwinds—ten to fifteen miles per hour—is ideal. If birds wait too long, they risk losing territories to more intrepid birds that already left. Without a territory, lollygaggers may not get a chance to mate. Conflicted, some gamble, hoping for the best. Some get lucky, finding temporary solace in cemeteries, city parks, and backyards. Others not so much, forced into the sea, a great lake, or skyscraper window.

Most songbirds prefer to migrate at night, taking advantage of predator-free skies. For orientation, many rely on a mysterious combination of celestial and magnetic cues. To keep track of each other on the wing, migrants make species-specific flight calls. If cloud cover keeps migrants low, an astute observer can hear several calls per second with ears cocked toward the heavens. Even better, if the moon is bright, silhouetted migrants can be counted as they pass in front of it. My cure for a numbers obsessed insomniac? Forget counting sheep and Sudoku. Count the fearless feathered specks ceaselessly hurling themselves through the spring night skies.

The most fearless of all may be the blackpoll warbler, a twelve-gram warbler with a black cap and a lot of ambition. These little forest dwellers winter in South America and breed in the boreal forests of North America. Unlike most sane warblers who work their way through Mexico and Central America on the way north each spring, blackpolls opt for a death-defying, three-day, nonstop flight over the Atlantic. Some touch down briefly in the eastern United States and then carry on all the way to their breeding grounds in Alaska. It is the longest migration of any New World warbler. After a short summer season raising a brood, blackpolls sense the days shortening and travel all the way back.

In a recent study headed by William DeLuca and the Vermont Center for Ecostudies, migrant blackpolls were fitted with miniature tracking devices—light-level geolocators—before their return departures. First, the birds doubled their weight. Then, those that took off from Nova Scotia or the Northeast flew south over the Atlantic to the Caribbean. After refueling in Hispaniola or Puerto Rico, they cruised across the Caribbean Sea to their wintering grounds in Columbia or Venezuela.

Albert Einstein suggested there are two ways to view life. One is to see nothing as a miracle. The other is to see everything as one. The blackpoll warbler, lighter than an empty soda can, launching itself 1,600 miles nonstop over the Atlantic seems to support the latter perspective. As does the thought that on any given night in May, tens of thousands of warblers are winging over my house as I sleep, all instinctual astronomers attuned to the Earth's magnetic field.

Fallouts seem miraculous too. While fallouts aren't too unusual, witnessing one is. My once-in-a-lifetime moment happened on an otherwise blah, overcast morning in May. Knowing it was spring migration, I had set an alarm and hoisted myself out of bed before light. Not long after, a half mile from the house, the drizzly morning turned dazzling. In an otherwise forgettable thicket danced dozens of glittery gems. Cape May, blackburnian, black-throated blue, magnolia, Nashville, hooded, bay-breasted . . . the warblers whirled around me like confetti. Laughing, I spun with the delirious dancers, ecstatic to have been invited to Renoir's *The Garden Party*.

My fallout had been a giddy affair. Liana's had been anything but. At least now I had the source of her downward spiral. But why had she so eagerly asked to have her journal returned?

I picked her journal off my desk and resumed reading. Sure enough, right after the film day, her mood and tone soured, matching her apathy I'd seen in class. After a low point, displayed in a distracted and truncated entry, her tone lightened. About a week later, verdant sprigs of optimism sprang up in her entries like trout lilies in March. Liana's last entry explained her resurgence:

> I've come to realize that I can enjoy nature and also be a balanced person. I don't have to let newfound interests dominate me. Just because I'm excited about something doesn't mean it has to own me. I look forward to finding new birds and adding them to my list all summer.

Such a simple yet profound epiphany that many of us fail to realize. Like most Hollywood films, *The Big Year* has a happy ending. And, fortunately for Liana, her newfound interest in birds may have one as well.

Golden-winged warbler

15 · A Golden Opportunity

Nature was a better teacher than school—and a lot more fun.

—Napoleon Bonaparte Broward

"Remember, if you see any splash of yellow, get our attention! Oh, and no talking and watch out for poison ivy. Let's move!" I barked my orders like a drill sergeant and my ornithology students obeyed with militaristic precision. Midway through my annual course, I pick a target bird—usually one that is rare or a habitat specialist—and we collectively seek it out. People love Holy Grail quests, I've found, regardless of their initial interest in the quarry. It seems to transform passive birdwatching into active bird-seeking, something my high-energy, college-age audiences tend to prefer. This year's target was the golden-winged warbler. It required an early wake-up and a three-hour drive to our current location at Bald Eagle State Park, in Pennsylvania.

The golden-winged warbler represents three things I love about birding. One, it's beautiful. Two, it's rare (at least where we live) making it memorable. And three, it likes a specific habitat—early successional forest adjacent to mature woods. The parents choose the regenerating weedy, brushy areas for their nests while their fledglings opt for deeper woods for predator evasion. Historically, such a habitat mosaic was created by natural disturbances, like fire. In the early twentieth century, settlers created even more, clearing land for farms and settlements. It was a golden period indeed for the warbler. It was also too good to be true. Woodlots regrew and farms consolidated and expanded. The Cornell Lab of Ornithology reports that since the 1960s, good golden-winged habitat in the Great Lakes region decreased by twenty-two percent. In the Appalachians, it plummeted forty-three percent.

All of these concepts and statistics were a trove of teachable moments, something I covet when teaching in the field. But my quest for rarity has an overwhelming downside—the prospect of not finding the target bird. As anybody who has ever pursued target birds well knows, there's a serious letdown that can accompany "dipping," or failing to find a sought-after species. While it's one thing to fail alone, it's quite another to fail corporately, especially when expectations are set and hopes are high. Group failure can transform me into the target—of criticism and lament. With such a grim prospect of failure in mind, I decided to embrace every avian gift we found. If we dipped on the golden-winged warbler, we'd at least have an impressive list. And Bald Eagle State Park in mid-May had plenty of gifts to bestow.

Fifty yards into our walk, we heard the unmistakable cries of alarmed killdeer. It's hard not to love killdeer, small sandpipers that often appear too elitist for muddy water. I love their mnemonic, homicidal name and that you don't have to get your feet muddy to see them. Best of all, I love their willingness to play charades. The closer we got to the bird, the more theatrical the killdeer became. Within minutes, the whole class had great looks at the classic broken-wing display I had described in class. Not only that, we found an egg-laden nest at our feet. Cameras clicked as we morphed into bird paparazzi. If the killdeer put up a performance like this, I thought, surely a golden-winged warbler would put in a cameo.

We left the parking lot and picked our way along good successional habitat. Gift after gift was given us. Willow flycatchers tipped back their heads to sing their strident songs like they were lining up for the limbo. Like the rest of the Tyrannidae family, willow flycatchers are suboscines, birds with vocal organs less developed than those of the oscine songbirds. It was ugly, like a Miley Cyrus song on repeat. But another teaching moment nonetheless. From other shrubs, eastern towhees reminded us to drink our tea. Even the park's namesake—a bald eagle—leered down at us as it soared languidly overhead. Our warm-up was now complete. It was time for the main event; time to see what we'd come for—a golden-winged warbler.

I looked at my watch. We had a little less than one hour left to find our target. Then we needed to head home. I picked up my pace.

"Let's try another locale," I suggested, trying not to sound nervous about the no-show. There were several nods and we trundled back to the vans and moved to our second spot, another early successional habitat within a nice chunk of more mature forest: a perfect patchwork. A squadron of blue-gray gnatcatchers soon heralded our hike. Their spastic antics commanded our attention as they bounced from branch to branch like pinballs. I enjoy gnatcatchers. But every minute we watched them was another minute we weren't searching for golden-wings. For the first time since leading groups in the field, I wanted—no, needed—the avian "extras" to pipe down.

But hooded warblers and ovenbirds heed no man's wishes in May. There are females to find, territories to stake out, and caterpillars to catch. Like the gnatcatchers, I loved these guys. But right now they were by-catch. Should I skip by such splendor? This was not a simple quantity versus quality dilemma. All of these birds were quality. Had I chosen the wrong target? Had I been foolish to select a target at all?

While my class savored the unsought bounty, I scanned for golden-wings to no avail. We had time for one more foray. "Let's try one last spot," I suggested, although my tone made it sound more like a command. Third time's a charm, I reminded myself. The chronic optimist in me refused to surrender. This day had to end with fluttery, golden wings.

We left the forest, "lost" more precious time on nesting cliff swallows under a bridge, and entered a shrubby thicket on a waterlogged trail. Time in the field always goes quickly. Today it was flying faster than the swallows. "Remember to shout out anything yellow you see. It's golden-winged or bust!" We slogged on.

"What's that?!" Seth, our class jock, had surprisingly taken a quick liking to birding. In a four-walled classroom, I was uncertain he had a pulse. But out here, he was alive and engaged. We all spun and followed the undulating flight of the small passerine. I knew that flight pattern.

"Female goldfinch!" I shouted, no longer willing to sacrifice the time it took to let students identify it. Instantly, everybody resumed walking. My tension had spread. Nobody spoke. Twenty yards ahead, I saw the undeniable flitting movement of a warbler. It had yellow and black and definite white wing bars. This had to be it! Now, we had to flush it out of the dense thicket. Channeling everything I had, I spished and squeaked with the intensity of two-dozen bath toys. With justified curiosity, the warbler poked its head out.

"Bin it!" I yelled. We all raised our bins. But I lowered mine just as quickly as I'd raised them. "Magnolia!" I said, sadly realizing this was the first time I'd ever been disappointed by such an exquisitely painted warbler. And this, I now realized, was the downside of the target bird approach.

"Well," I said morosely, "I think we need to head back. We're already late."

"We can't!" Seth demanded. "We're going to find this bird!" The whole class turned to scrutinize him. Even now, after two hours in the hot sun, no lunch, and a three-hour van trip, Seth wanted to keep going. He met our gaze, pumped his fist, and smiled. For good or ill, Seth was not to be denied this quest. And this never-say-die attitude that sometimes emerges epitomizes all that is right with the target bird approach. This was a game and Seth—a born competitor—was determined to win.

I glanced from face to face, searching for consensus. Brittany stepped forward. "I think I saw a golden-winged warbler back on the trail."

"Why didn't you get our attention?" I implored, somewhat exasperated.

"Because I wasn't sure until now." She stoically met my gaze.

"Describe its field marks." I was skeptical.

"Well, it was small and yellow with a black bib and had wing bars."

"That does suggest a golden-wing," I said. "But how far back on the trail?"

"Just down there." She motioned to a nearby clump of young cottonwoods.

"That decides it!" Seth chimed in, sliding past people to beeline for the grove. We all fell in step and I felt energy surge through the group. Even my own heart was racing. This was turning out better than expected with a classic happily-ever-after ending. It would be a buzzer-beater finish; we'd find the coveted warbler just as time expired. And Seth and Brittany—a hero and heroine—had emerged to fulfill the quest. My role as unrelenting whip-cracker had morphed; now I was a follower, last in line, and elated that the mantle of motivation had been passed to those who were better at it.

Two hundred yards down the trail Brittany stopped our stampede and motioned toward a few red maple saplings. We fanned out through the knee-high brush. If there was indeed a golden-wing in here, our phalanx would surely find it. "I think I have Brittany's bird!" yelled Anne, a lanky and normally laconic student. Now well trained, we zeroed in on a particularly scrawny sapling. My heart leapt. There at the top was a gorgeous yellow bird with a black bib and white wing bars. It spiraled up the tree like a strand of DNA and posed perfectly at the apex. Yes indeed, we had finally found a . . . female orchard oriole.

My heart sank faster than a piano dropped into a lake. It was my responsibility to break the news. "This," I stated dryly, "is as close as you can come to seeing a golden-winged warbler without actually seeing one." Nobody laughed.

"You mean it's not one?" Brittany said disbelievingly.

"It's an orchard oriole," I replied, "which is a pretty awesome bird." But like the goldfinch and magnolia warbler before, the orchard oriole was not our target. Its awesomeness—and unique status as North America's smallest member of the Icteridae family—could not suffice.

"This was totally worth it!" I motioned for Anne to lead us back to the vans. Try as I might, my enthusiasm felt as hollow as our rumbling stomachs. I swung my bins to the side and let dejected silence descend.

A nice lunch at a local diner soothed our spirits but couldn't erase the unmistakable fact that we all knew too well—we had failed in our quest. Trusting that distraction could ease our distraught state, I cranked the radio up on the long drive home and racked my brain. No, we hadn't found our target bird. But we had found so many other avian treasures. All of which resulted from our quest. By the time I walked into class the next morning, my mental metamorphosis was complete.

"I'm glad we didn't find the golden-winged warbler," I led off matter-of-factly. A sea of blank faces met my own. Nobody said a word. Satisfied with the confusion I'd created, I continued.

"If we had found it, I bet some of you would never look for it again. Since we didn't, I know a few of you will keep searching." A few people smirked, indicating that I'd reasoned correctly. As I'd noticed with Seth in the field, the questers in the class would keep questing; they were wired that way. It was as natural as breathing. They had to. I continued my monologue.

"While it'd be great to find a golden-wing one day, it's the search that's significant. It keeps us learning and more importantly, it keeps us going out. As you saw yesterday, the journey is laden with gems, like killdeer and flycatchers and orioles. And think how much more joy you'll have one day, when your search finally bears it out. Failure keeps us searching. And it makes the joy more complete."

About once a semester, my words actually come out as I intend. This was one of those rare times. I ended my speech, shuffled back to the blackboard, and commenced a lecture about bird anatomy. This semester's quest may have ended. But some of my students would soon embark on quests of their own. Maybe even to the Appalachians in Pennsylvania. Why? Because in a game of hide-and-seek, being "it" isn't all that bad. You may not find exactly who you're looking for. Whomever you find—and the joy you find seeking—will more than make up for it.

16 · LITTLE PINK BUNDLES

Joanna Macy writes that until we can grieve for our planet we cannot love it—grieving is a sign of spiritual health. But it is not enough to weep for our lost landscapes; we have to put our hands in the earth to make ourselves whole again. Even a wounded world is feeding us. Even a wounded world holds us, giving us moments of wonder and joy. I choose joy over despair.

—Robin Wall Kimmerer, *Braiding Sweetgrass*

"Can you identify this bird for me?" the subject line of a friend's email succinctly asked. My cursor sped over and clicked the photo attachment. This was a chance to identify a bird, help a friend, and possibly stroke my ego all at once. Way too tempting to pass up. The requests for recommendation letters and summaries of committee meetings could wait.

The photo showed a large brown raptor tearing at what appeared to be a deer carcass. Under the photo were my friend Jeff's words: "Saw this on my way back from lunch today. Some kind of hawk, right?"

I smiled and hit reply. This low-hanging fruit required neither contemplation nor reference books. "Immature bald eagle," I wrote back, wishing my entire inbox was bird identification requests. Knowing Jeff was typically far busier than I was, I figured our exchange was over. It wasn't. A few minutes later, he replied.

"Seemed too small to be an eagle. I usually see red-tails around this place. Are you sure it's an eagle?"

I was sure. I was also a little hurt. As a professor, I was no stranger to incredulity and even the occasional pointed challenge from a student. For some reason, it stung a little bit coming from Jeff. Perhaps because I considered birds to be my thing, the one subject I had down. I clicked back on the earlier attachment, rechecked the field marks, and fired back another email, making sure to conceal my wounded pride. It was a young eagle, I explained, pointing out the huge size difference compared to the adjacent crow also feeding at the carcass. I also mentioned the flecks of white starting to show along the eagle's throat and nape. The classic white head of a bald eagle doesn't appear until year four.

Despite my list of field marks, I still doubted Jeff believed me. His lack of response confirmed my suspicion. Even so, I didn't lose any sleep. When it comes to eagles, there's plenty to be incredulous about. As our nation's symbol, we're used to thinking of them as massive, regal, white-headed birds that snatch fish with aplomb. Reality has a way of complicating our stereotypes, however. The reality is that bald eagles may not be as regal as we'd like. One, they're klepto-parasites. This means they're just as happy to steal food as they are to catch it themselves. Two, they're not above eating roadkill or any rotten remains they happen to fly over. And three, they can look pretty scruffy in their adolescence. I can't help but think that Benjamin Franklin's turkey would have made a slightly more virtuous symbol.

Wild turkeys do share something with eagles. Something far more important than the lopsided contest to represent our nation. Both species are great illustrations of a profoundly important concept in conservation biology. A concept that I think best explains Jeff's lingering doubt as to whether the bird he saw was really an eagle. In 1995, fisheries scientist Daniel Pauly coined the term "shifting baselines syndrome" to describe a phenomenon scientists observed regarding the world's plummeting fish populations. Although scientists were well aware that fish stocks were sinking, few seemed to capture the full extent of the decline. The reason, Pauly noted, is that each generation of scientist tended to measure the decline from the level it was when they began their careers.

It's not just scientists, of course, who get duped. We all do. Peter H. Kahn Jr. suggests that each of us constructs a conception of what is environmentally normal based upon what we encounter in childhood. Environmental degradation perpetually increases. But each subsequent generation, Kahn says, takes the degraded condition as a non-degraded one. What each generation perceives as a normal baseline really isn't. As a result, comprehensive losses across generations never come into focus. Why? Because as Jon Mooallem writes in *Wild Ones*, each generation of scientists is focused on only one small part of the line of the graph. And unfortunately, the line representing wildlife populations is dropping like Wile E. Coyote after stupidly sprinting off a cliff.

Depending on what time in history you examine the populations of turkeys and eagles, you could easily deduce a similarly distorted picture. For much of my life, for example, turkeys have been a common species. I see them regularly in hayfields, highway medians, even just outside my living room window. They were also common for Native Americans, on the order of about ten million pre-Columbian birds. But as America was colonized and human populations grew, so too did the demand for turkey. Unregulated hunting combined with habitat loss caused the turkey to disappear from eighteen of the thirty-nine states it had originally occupied. Numbers dropped to around two hundred thousand, a ninety percent reduction from their pre-Columbian level.

If I had been born in 1940 like my father, the low point for turkey populations, seeing one would have been a fantastically rare event. As a kid, my dad never saw turkeys. The opposite was true for my childhood; turkeys were everywhere. In just one generation, the baseline had shifted incredibly. What makes it so noteworthy, is that unlike the baselines of many other species, this one shifted positively. The baseline has shifted similarly with eagles, but this time it's been between my generation and my children's.

Back in 1782, when the eagle was declared our national symbol, it is thought there were about 50,000 pairs soaring the skies. Despite the raptor's lofty status, Americans promptly embarked on a wanton killing spree, degrading habitats through deforestation and pesticide use. By 1960, just 400 nesting pairs were left in the lower forty-eight (on the bright side, golden-winged warblers were booming; such is the nuanced nature of habitat conversion). Unless hailing from the Pacific Northwest or Florida, the likelihood for any baby boomer to see our national symbol in the wild was, at this point, virtually nil. The precipitous loss was so great that even President John F. Kennedy weighed in, writing: "The fierce beauty and proud independence of this great bird symbolizes the strength and freedom of America. But as latter-day citizens we shall fail our trust if we permit the eagle to disappear."

The Endangered Species Act arrived in the nick of time. When the Act was finally signed in 1973, the bald eagle was one of the first officially placed on it. A combination of regulatory restrictions, nesting site protections, and reintroduction programs contributed to a dramatic recovery. By 1995, the lower forty-eight's population had climbed from 400 to 4,700 nesting pairs.

For my friend Jeff and I in the late 1990s, this still wasn't enough to make eagles a common sight. Our baselines had ossified over our youth; to us, bald eagles remained a rarely seen species. But by 2007, the year my son was born, the number of eagles climbed from 4,700 to over 10,000 pairs and the eagle was delisted from the endangered species list. In the midst of their soaring population, they recolonized our region in western New York.

With one eye always skyward, I soon began seeing eagles regularly for the first time in my life. For a while, it was about once a month. Now, it's almost weekly. There are so many eagles around that I often feel cheated if a few days go by and I don't see one. My childhood baseline has finally shifted. But others less birdbrained may not have noticed this shift yet. Or, they're not quite ready to accept it. For them, red-tailed hawks remain the likely species at a roadside carcass. This, I suspect, lay at the heart of Jeff's reluctance to believe my ID.

Shifting baselines syndrome also lies at the heart of a vexing conservation problem. The syndrome, which Kahn also dubbed "environmental generational amnesia," basically means that we have no objective criterion by which to assess the health of wildlife populations. Is 10,000 nesting pairs of eagles really a miraculous recovery? Or is this, as Mooallem writes, "just a meager uptick after a much longer, more devastating decline?" Should we really delist them? What baseline should we use? Are we forever doomed to wallow in a pit of ecological subjectivity?

When I think about the problem of shifting baselines syndrome and the host of other seemingly intractable conservation problems our current generation is mired in, it's easy for me to become a glass half-empty guy. I was entertaining such a cocktail of sour thoughts when I walked into my shed last summer to look for an old car jack. What happened in the span of a minute changed the tenor of my teaching and maybe even my entire outlook on life. So moved, I twice volunteered sharing this incredible story with friends. And twice, you'll soon see why, I was kindly told it's better told elsewhere. Here is my elsewhere.

Upon entering the overstuffed shed, I lifted a dusty, deflated duffle bag. Woodchips and paper shreds fell to the floor like confetti. In the place where the duffle bag had been was a wide-eyed mouse. Not only was the mouse wide-eyed, it was also pregnant. So pregnant, in fact, that a fresh pink baby emerged from its watery womb right before my eyes. Maybe pet shop owners are accustomed to such phenomena. I certainly wasn't.

Justifiably startled by having her neonatal roof removed so suddenly, the birthing mother mouse launched onto the floor of my shed, squirted between my legs, and headed out the open door and into the yard. Mice apparently have trouble halting the birth process midstream, or at least this one did. Every three feet, a naked pink baby was unceremoniously ejected into the grass like Hansel and Gretel leaving a trail of breadcrumbs.

Although weighing just 0.05 ounces, each newborn baby immediately commenced squeaking, high pitched and pitifully. I bent down and examined one. One third the size of my pinky finger and immobile, I knew it wouldn't last an hour exposed to the elements. Despite my lifetime spent trying to annihilate mice, here I was suddenly wondering how I could save these seconds-old sausage links. I didn't have to wonder for long.

In a moment, the mother, the very one that had disappeared into the yard, marched back for her babies. When she reached the first, she lifted it with her teeth and carried it into the brush with all of the tenderness of a lioness moving a cub. If the mother mouse was scared of my towering frame, she never showed it; all her focus was on securing her little pink bundles of life. Forty-five seconds and three determined trips later, the life-saving spectacle was over.

As a parent, I understand devotion to offspring. As an ecologist, I also understand that parental devotion is linked to parental investment. For long-lived mammals with long gestation periods, it's unsurprising a mother will stop at nothing to protect a baby. That's what threw me with the mouse. Deer mice are profligate breeders. Gestation is less than one month and they reproduce six to ten times per year. Multiplied by the average litter size of four babies, that's about thirty-two babies per year per female. Knowing this, I figured the mother would cut her losses, turn tail, and run. After all, she could be pregnant again in the time it would take me to walk back into the house. And before I'd finished painting the back deck, she could have a fresh new litter.

But something deep in that little mouse's DNA told her otherwise. Rather than run, she spun around on her delicate rodent paws in broad daylight and braved the dumbstruck biped. Instinct, empathy, whatever it was, she would not leave her offspring unprotected without a fight. Reepicheep was real indeed.

My students also sometimes seem like little pink bundles left on the grass; my children even more so. We've dropped them abruptly and unceremoniously into a mess. Inveterate problems like exploding human populations, climate change, habitat conversion, biodiversity loss, invasive species, and yes, shifting baselines syndrome. The parade of pressures is as paralyzing as it is long. It's easy to become pessimistic and hopelessly cynical. It's even easier for me to pass hopelessness onto my students and my kids. How can I convey to them that Chicken Little was right, that the sky really is falling? And do so in a way that doesn't make them even wearier with conservation fatigue? If my students raise the white flag . . . well, conservation doesn't stand a chance.

For now my solution is simple. I'm going to tell turkey tales.

I'll tell anybody who will listen that a turkey squadron seventeen strong trudged through the snow in my yard a few weeks ago. Seventeen! And that had I been born when my grandparents or my parents were, I wouldn't have seen any. Zero.

Then I'll move on to the eagle. I'll skip the part about why it's probably not our best choice as a national symbol. I'll focus instead on the fact that while I rarely saw them growing up, my kids now see them all the time. Baselines have shifted. And for these two species at least, things are looking up. No, I don't want this generation to grow more complacent than it already has. I don't want them feeling hopeless and helpless either. If Emily Dickinson was right about hope being the thing with feathers, well . . . we sure need something to perch in our soul these days.

Dian Fossey had hope. It is what motivated her to defend her little pink bundles, the mountain gorillas in East Africa. In the last entry of her diary before she was murdered by poachers at her field camp in 1985, she wrote: "If you realize the value of all life, you dwell less on what is past and concentrate more on the preservation of the future." Fossey's prescient words are more important now than ever. They are why I am choosing to trumpet the few gains in lieu of the legion of losses. I've decided that for however many years I have left on this planet, seeking to save my own skin isn't enough. I'm going all out for the little pink bundles on the grass. And as I do, I may even send one more follow-up email to my friend, Jeff. Two sentences will suffice: That was no hawk, man. Believe me, it was an eagle.

17 · THE DEONTOLOGICAL BIRDER

Reality is unforgivingly complex.

—Anne Lamott

I like to teach ornithology. I crave it, actually. Fundamental concepts like synchronous hatching and brood parasitism are balm to my soul. If I spy any literature on birds, from a soiled brochure to a multi-volume encyclopedia, I devour it with alacrity. I have a birdbrain: my occipital lobe records our feathered friends at the expense of everything else, my temporal lobe ferrets out avian-related facts, and my hippocampus caches it all away like a scrub jay does acorns. Teaching ornithology feels effortless, like a hawk riding thermals. So naturally, I welcome questions and look forward to the earnestly raised hand.

"What bird was that?" Mason asked, flagging me with a raised pen as my class stood around me in a clearing in the woods.

"A scarlet tanager," I replied, wishing the ravishing red bird with jet-black wings would give us one more flyover. Mason scribbled the name into his journal and looked back at me, making no effort to conceal ongoing puzzlement.

"Come to think of it, what is a tanager?" He glanced around at the eleven other far less curious students. I smiled. This was a moment I loved: an earnest student, a sunny May morning, and an easy, softball question. Unlike the other courses I taught, in

141

this one I was confidently full of answers.

"A tanager is any member of the Thraupidae family." I tried to conceal the poignant pleasure I felt displaying my arcane knowledge. I had hardly worked to memorize the 234 bird families the world boasts; I just read them a few times and they stuck. Finally, knowledge that was so profoundly useless in every other aspect of life seemed meaningful and pertinent. I couldn't resist continuing. "We have four tanagers in the US: the hepatic, the summer, the western, and the one you just saw—the scarlet—who lives here in the Northeast. They've divvied up the continent like a bunch of colonial imperialists. The summer claims the Southeast, the hepatic the Southwest, and the western, well, that's obvious." I paused, wondering if I'd overwhelmed my students. Half were madly scribbling while the rest—the Type Bs—were staring dreamily into the canopy.

Except for Mason. He did neither, opting instead to stare at me with a furrowed brow. Obviously he wasn't downloading my barrage of tanager data. "Did I confuse you?" I asked, wondering why we weren't connecting.

"What I mean is," Mason said, pulling the end of his pen out of his mouth, "what is a tanager?" He drew out the "is," emphasizing it with a higher pitch.

"Well, like I said, it's any songbird in the Thraupidae family." Maybe Mason simply needed more info. "If you travel south to the New World tropics, you'll encounter hordes—over two hundred—of different tanager species. But . . . it's a problematic family. Some experts want them reclassified due to new molecular evidence. A few species may be moved into the Fringillidae, the finches, while others, like the scarlet we just saw, may get put into the cardinal family. It's all in flux. In fact, I think the American Ornithologists' Union already did reclassify them." My tanager knowledge was now kaput. Surely this cleared up Mason's quandary.

His unchanged expression revealed little progress. We were at a logjam. Mason's simple four-word question had blown apart my artifice of knowledge. My enthusiasm, overflowing when I began, had drained away like a pond behind a broken beaver dam.

Conflict-hater Stephanie, who had silently observed our give-and-take like a tennis match, recognized the need for a translator. "What Mason means is, what are the key characteristics of a tanager?"

"Yeah," Mason agreed. "What is it?" All writing ceased as everybody, even the daydreamers, turned to watch me. The class recognized salience. Now, with the suddenness of a lightning strike, I realized the obvious: I was stumped. This question, arguably the most fundamental of any ornithology course, left me wordless, thoughtless even. Here in the only course I had any confidence in, I was a fledgling. One that, despite a lot of flapping, had whacked into a tree. Like several disconcerting times before, I had to admit my ignorance.

"You know what, Mason, I guess I don't know what a tanager is. I'll have to think about it." While I doubted my students sensed it, I had plunged into a mini existential crisis. Did I actually know anything? Was I equipped for any profession?

Silence ensued. A long, heavy silence. Fortunately, a Thoreau quote fluttered by. I grabbed it. Like bird families and factoids, I carried an arsenal of easy-to-fire quotes. They were inspirational and at times like this, good for redirecting awkward moments. "Have any of you heard what Thoreau said about tanagers?" I asked, confident they hadn't. "The tanager flies through the green foliage as if it would ignite the leaves." Chins went up and gazes returned to the treetops. For now, the pressure was off.

Thoreau's tanager may have ignited the leaves but Mason's

tanager did something far more important: it ignited the depths of my ignorance, exposing my hubris. It has trailed me like a lonely dog ever since. With a life full of distraction and duty, I'd let it go dormant. But a recent hike with an old friend, Dustin, resurrected my ignorance in an eerily similar way.

"Hey, look." I pointed ahead of us on the trail. "A varied thrush."

"Cool," Dustin replied. "Looks like a robin." Dustin was cut of the same cloth as Mason; rarely was he content to swim along the surface. I wasn't surprised by his next question.

"What's a thrush?"

"Well, it's any bird in the Turdidae family . . ." I stopped short but it was too late. Smoke and mirrors wouldn't work here. Dustin was too shrewd.

"It's an ontological question," he clarified, although I'd already guessed as much. I was hiking behind Dustin. But I could feel his smirk. For a brief moment, I considered commandeering the rest of our hike with a canned lecture about bird classification, homologous and derived characteristics, and cladistics. A misguided monologue would punish him for his impudence. As before with Mason, this wasn't the solution. Dustin preferred ultimate questions. Philosophical questions laced with theological underpinnings.

"You'll have to ask God, then," I remarked sourly, knowing I'd lost this latest bout of mental jousting; jousting I typically reveled in. Not this time. This one had opened up a wound. Thrusting my hands in my pockets, I changed the subject.

Ignorance, for me, rarely feels like bliss. Like any person with a smidgeon of self-esteem, I loathe displaying it. With Mason and Dustin, however, I'd done so in a subject I purportedly understood; one I professed. According to Merriam-Webster, ontology is a branch of metaphysics that deals with the nature and relations of being, or an organizational system to help explain relationships. In some ways, it's like a sibling of taxonomy and systematics, except it's more existential and mysterious.

The more I've researched the subject, the more I've come to realize that I have no ontological clue what a tanager or a thrush is. None of my myriad reference books help either. I can describe them and provide a litany of facts and quotes, but, as I clearly showed before, that's the end of it. After that, all I can do is posit and theorize. Perhaps Plato was right in his *Allegory of the Cave*. Perhaps all that I think I know about a tanager is mere opinion, mere shadows on the cave wall. Perhaps real knowledge—the kind Mason and Dustin sought—can only be attained through philosophical inquiry. Admitting the limits of my knowledge may have been the best answer—and the most honest—I could have given.

Such honest moments of ignorance sure punch holes in my pride, though. A quick detour into philosophy reveals that right or wrong, my damaged ego is a consequence of my action, that of admitting my limitations. This, according to the ethics of deontology, does not affect the rightness or the wrongness of the action itself. If I lean into deontology and let go of consequentialism, therefore, my pride should be rendered irrelevant. So stating my ignorance is morally good regardless of my injured self-esteem. As Immanuel Kant would agree, this is acting on moral law, a categorical imperative.

Even that little jaunt into philosophy makes my birdbrain swirl around like a fickle flock of starlings. Dabbling in it makes me wonder if I'll ever comprehend the essence of a tanager. This doesn't diminish my fondness for ornithology, though. After all, most of my students seem satisfied with bird families, factoids, and quotes. But one thing I'll change. When the next student wants something deeper, I'll spare them a misguided monologue and tout my ignorance with far less shame. Why?

Because as I'm sure Plato and Kant would agree, it's folly for a simpleton like me to expatiate on the metaphysics of ontology. It's categorically imperative I refrain. Consequentialism is inauspicious. Deontologically speaking, of course.

18 · Serendipitous Birding

> *To the scientist Nature is a storehouse of facts, laws, processes; to the artist she is a storehouse of pictures; to the poet she is a storehouse of images, fancies, a source of inspiration; to the moralist she is a storehouse of precepts and parables; to all she may be a source of knowledge and joy.*
>
> —John Burroughs

"Eli, here's my bird journal." Tess handed me a small, nondescript brown notebook. "But you need to read this letter first," she added, pulling a neatly folded piece of paper from her pocket. "This explains my pathetic journal. I hope you won't think less of me for it."

"I'm sure I won't." I stuffed the letter into my back pocket. "Thanks, Tess."

I thought nothing more of it, used as I was to getting hastily written notes of excuse or explanation from desperate students at the end of semesters. But Tess wasn't a desperate student merely hoping to pass a class. She excelled in all the courses I offered. She was tall, with long dirty-blond hair and eyes that spoke of unceasing analysis of the world around her. Nearly every morning that I'd seen her on our study abroad semester in Tanzania, she had been sitting out in the open, staring at the treetops. Unlike other students who were always doing something, Tess often wasn't. She was content to be. As a teacher living in constant community with your students, you notice these things.

The wildlife behavior course that I taught had gone well. Not because of me—because of Tanzania. Unlike other African countries that have seen their wildlife diminish due to increasing habitat loss and land conversion, Tanzania is still packed with megafauna, the charismatic animals that also populate screen savers, *National Geographic*, and Disney movies. Its bountiful birds catch the eye of even the most disinterested of students. As part of the grade, each student is required to see one hundred birds during their time there—an easily obtainable goal even for beginners. If accomplished, I remind them, they've seen roughly one percent of the world's bird species. I encourage students not to stop even if they hit one hundred. As incentive, I offer a reward to whomever finds the most species. In years past, it has developed into a healthy competition during which students zealously guard their lists and go birding a lot. So I've stuck with it. It's a fun way to get the students into nature, give them something they can be proud of, and shed light on the incredible diversity of bird species in our world.

At least, I thought it was fun. Tess most definitely did not. Somewhat unwittingly, she had been pegged by many of the other students to win the competition. Everybody realized that Tess was a natural birder. More than that, everybody wanted her to beat Josh. Josh was the quintessential competitive jock (not unlike Seth, who'd rallied our charge for the golden-winged warbler back in Pennsylvania). If there was a contest, Josh had to win it. So, when I announced the contest, Josh accepted it with alacrity, aided by a camera with a large telephoto lens. Before the contest was announced, he'd had little interest in birds. Afterward, he sought birds round the clock. Every morning, he woke up early and chased the local birds like a caffeine addict does coffee. But Josh, like many beginning birders, quickly realized that many birds in Tanzania—or anywhere—are difficult to tell apart. He was not about to let this little obstacle foil him. Instead of using binoculars, Josh took photos, lots of photos. One day, near the beginning of the contest, he approached me. "Would you have time to help me name some of the birds I've seen?"

"Can you describe them?" I expected him to launch into a long paragraph of description along the lines of "it had a brown body, black head, orange legs . . ."

"I don't need to. They're on my camera," he responded matter-of-factly.

Before the contest started, I had laid out the ground rules. For a species to count, it has to be alive, unrestrained, and seen. I had never said anything about cameras. And now, Josh was relying almost entirely on his. Tess, armed with little more than a point-and-shoot, could not. And philosophically, she would not. She was, I was learning, a different kind of student and a different kind of birder.

The other students realized what Josh was doing and realized they didn't have a chance against him. One by one, they found their required one hundred species and dropped out of the contest. Josh snapped every bird he saw, even small specks on the horizon. Then, with a bird book, or me next to him, he zoomed in on his LCD screen and identified each bird. Josh was "seeing" numerous birds, even species I hadn't ever seen despite spending more than a decade in the country. They were little feathered, flighty specks out in the field, but his camera made them large and cooperative. More often than not, I could identify them instantly. And so, they went on his list.

As it often goes in contests, if you can't win yourself, then you get behind someone who can. Preferably, someone you agree with. Even more preferably, an underdog. Tess was just that unwitting underdog. Each day, her classmates cornered her: "Tess, how many birds do you have? Are you up to 200 yet? Josh is up to 203! But you can beat him!"

I was conflicted. I admired Josh's drive and ambition. But his style was questionable. I wondered if he was really developing field observation skills. He hadn't done anything wrong per se. He was simply exploiting a loophole in the rules. Unwilling to retroactively change the contest's parameters, I let it continue unabated. Most everybody had reached the one-hundred-bird goal and started cheering Tess on. Josh was more determined than ever. He forged ahead with his camera, regardless of the absence of a cheerleading section. Even with all the moral support, Tess hadn't changed her methodology. Each morning she sat faithfully in her chair with binoculars wrapped round her neck like an Olympic medal. She didn't seem any worse for the wear, at least outwardly.

The final day arrived and all the students turned in their completed bird journals. All but two found at least 100 species. Not bad at all. Then I opened Josh's and looked at his total: 306. Wow! I had to give him credit. As a student, I had found a mere 167. Tess's journal was right under Josh's. I opened it. Although I had tried to remain impartial, I, too, was sort of hoping she had beaten him. Her journal was a work of art. Exquisite sketches and portrayals of birds with accompanying field notes. Each page could be framed, the kind of product only born of patient observation.

Still anxious to know her total, I paged through it carefully and counted the birds. One hundred. No more. No less. Good enough for an A on the assignment. But it seemed like an empty A. The journal was lovely, but I had expected more birds. I wanted more. I closed it and reached for my grade book. Then I remembered the letter. I pulled it out of my back pocket. Tess's words leapt off the page:

Dear Eli, I love birds, always have, but I like to know them—

not just sight them and check them off a list. I don't count birds. In fact, the very notion appalls me in a way I cannot hope to describe. With that mindset, birding becomes a personal accomplishment rather than a relationship with nature. Where is the learning, the growing understanding, in glimpsing a feathery friend and having someone shout out its moniker in your general direction? Or in snapping an impersonal photo to later compare to an impersonal illustration in a book into which someone else poured his life and research? It is a great frustration that a passion for living creatures is forced to turn into a brutal competition. Since day one, people have been demanding knowledge of my number of birds and egging me on to 'beat' everyone else—the very thought of which disgusts me. I confess to sitting and watching a single bird or small flocks for extensive periods of time just to get in their heads. Lisa [another professor] calls this 'serendipitous birding' and I am rather fond of the term. The eyes are never large enough, nor the brain quick enough to take in all the information that I yearn for.

I read the letter. And reread it. The idea Tess was conveying wasn't new to me. But never had I seen it so artfully and cogently stated. To list or not to list—that is the question.

Competitive birding versus serendipitous birding. Renowned birder Kenn Kaufman has done both, and he's dubbed Tess's style an "Epic Year" rather than a "Big Year." An Epic Year is geared toward learning about the birds you're seeing—knowing them—while a Big Year is geared more toward counting and competing.

Although Tess's letter was beautifully conceived and her point well taken, I'm not convinced it has to be an either/or. I, for one, enjoy both knowing the birds and counting them—even competing. And, although there may be seasons in a birder's life for each, I think one can also do them simultaneously. In fact, back when I began birding in my early teens, I began as a knower, developed an interest in listing, and now do both. Roger Tory Peterson, the bird guru himself, claimed many people go from looker to listing to scientist.

I wrote an A on Tess's paper, folded up her letter, and put it in my wallet. It was a keeper. Occasionally I've pulled it out and let her words sink in anew.

Last winter, I put Tess's ideas into practice. While driving along a country road in rural New York, I chanced upon a huge flock of snow buntings. Thousands of them. In Africa during the winter months, snow buntings were a rare treat. I sat in my truck squinting through the falling snow, yearning to insert myself into the flock. Despite the blustery late December cold, the roadside didn't suffice. Like me, the black-and-white birds couldn't make up their minds, swirling in dizzying numbers all around an agricultural field. All over the field, the thin layer of snow was besmeared with something light gray. An old farmhouse sat under a few gnarly bare trees a half-mile away. It was Sunday afternoon. Surely the farmer had his feet up in a recliner watching an NFL game. Walking out in the field wouldn't hurt anything, especially in winter. How close would the bunting flock let me come? Decision made, I got out of my truck and slowly walked out toward the flock.

The buntings seemed to be enjoying a Sabbath, too. Unconcerned, they let me approach, hundreds alighting just a few yards away. Enthralled, I dropped down on all fours, and shot eye-level photos, pointing my lens in all directions as the capricious birds exploded into the air and landed again, rarely with any warning.

My knees soaked and cold, I stood up. I glanced over at my truck. Just behind it was a red truck. A man climbed out and came my way. Oh no. Busted. Trespassing without permission.

The birds had done it again.

Despite the cold, the middle-aged man wore a green baseball cap with a heavily creased brim. His hands were tucked into the pockets of his grease-stained Carhartt coat. Something about his walk seemed odd. It was hesitant, defeated even. At about ten feet away he stopped. I tensed, waiting for the inevitable—probably a profanity-riddled reprimand. What he said, however, disarmed me entirely.

"Sorry."

"Sorry for what?" I asked.

"I only sprayed just this once," he said, avoiding eye contact. Then it hit me like a stone. This guy had done something untoward. And now he thought I was from some regulatory commission, like the EPA. For a brief nefarious second, I considered playing along.

"I'm just looking at your great birds." I motioned toward the still swirling flocks. The man lifted his gaze, looking out.

"You mean those?" Now able to see under his brim, I saw the confusion in his eyes.

"Yeah, I've never seen so many snow buntings ever," I replied matter-of-factly. "Just had to get a better look, and some photos." The man looked at my camera and then again at the birds. As it had me, understanding dawned on him. His eyebrows went up. Both of us, for totally different reasons, had assumed to be upbraided. "Do you mind if I take a few more photos?" I asked hopefully. "I'm from the next town over," I added, hoping to assuage him more.

"Shoot all you want!" he replied, his face now light. "They come and go all winter. Love it when I spray manure for 'em. Pretty little things, eh?"

"Sure are," I replied. "And uh, sorry for just walking right in here. I know it . . ."

"Whenever you like," he said, cutting me off. He tipped his

hat and headed back to his truck. A strong gust whipped by, but even the increasing gale couldn't darken my mood. Yes, I had seen snow buntings before. I hadn't come out here for my list. Today, I'd wanted to know buntings better, figure out what makes them tick. And in a dumb stroke of luck, I'd been able to do just that. Yes, I had a camera. But it was documenting more than birds. It was documenting serendipity.

19 · PLEASE DISTURB

I have read many definitions of what is a conservationist, and written not a few myself, but I suspect that the best one is written not with a pen, but with an axe. It is a matter of what a man thinks about while chopping, or while deciding what to chop. A conservationist is one who is humbly aware that with each stroke he is writing his signature on the face of his land.

—Aldo Leopold

Class was quickly taking on the feel of a forced march. Energy levels were flagging, black flies were buzzing, and the swamp's morning bird symphony had reached a quiet intermission. As an overly optimistic professor, I desperately wanted my students to see a northern goshawk, the fierce and elusive bird of our northern forests.

I turned to my sunbaked audience, hoping to rouse them for one last pursuit. "We'll leave the swamp and head into this grove of evergreens!" I exhorted, hoping my voice would carry to those in the back. "But first let's switch disciplines. Let's talk conservation bio for a moment. Who can tell me why we need large expanses of intact forest?"

Fortunately, at least one student, Joe, remained lucid. "Because that's the only place that some species will use."

"Exactly." I flashed him an appreciative smile. "The goshawk is a case in point."

The canopy closed overhead as we marched into the evergreens. Last year, I had staked out a place that goshawks had historically nested in. Now, as we marched, I noticed sunlight coming from my desired destination. What had happened to my forest? Like many who frequent public lands, I felt informal ownership of this parcel.

Moments later, to my dismay, the mystery solved itself. The previous year's goshawk grounds had been transformed into a clear-cut, the ground littered with fallen treetops and bramble. The forest surrounding the clear-cut was still intact, though, as if aliens had flown over and sucked up a perfectly rectangular patch for further study.

The students read my expression like a book. "I guess we won't be finding any goshawks, will we?" a girl asked.

"Not today," I responded, feebly trying to mask my despair. I paused a moment to collect myself. I couldn't. Like the Lorax, my dander was up. My emotions bubbled up and I stood on my soapbox, made possible by a nearby stump. I knew better than to intentionally interject my own biases into my class. But I was too wounded to refrain. "This," I exclaimed, "is what happens when you clear-cut before consulting with ornithologists, ecologists, and conservation biologists! Yeah, it'll grow back. But goshawks don't tolerate ripped up forests. They need their home intact. Maybe they've found suitable nesting nearby. But I doubt it. Look at this, everybody, and remember it . . ."

I paused, hoping to impregnate the moment with meaning and inspire the next generation of environmentalists. Stunned by my outburst, nobody said a word. But the silence was broken by an unmistakable warble. At first it was faint. I cupped my ears. Like an approaching ambulance, the beautiful string of notes steadily increased.

"What is that?" Joe scanned the vegetation with his binoculars.

Here was a prize student indeed.

"It's a warbler." I tried to hide my uncertainty.

I needed time to flip through my dusty mental audio database and retrieve this species, one I hadn't heard, or seen, in years. But Joe was persistent. My students detested hypocrisy. Professors who professed philosophy from freshly hacked tree stumps had better be able to profess the name of a dainty little bird warbling nearby.

My dimly flickering light bulb blazed. "It's a mourning warbler!"

I crashed through a tangle, absorbed a dozen blackberry thorns, and finally laid eyes on the little yellow bird sporting an indigo hood. Sure enough, a male mourning warbler was singing his heart out from the top of a small sapling. "Do you all see it?" I whisper-shouted back to my confused class.

A few heads nodded; others madly scanned the foliage. The warbler dissolved back into the dappled brush. Excited, I fought my way back to the class and dredged up my memorized ream of mourning warbler facts.

"Now that is a fantastic bird!" I began. "It's never widespread because of its very specific habitat requirements. It wants a disturbed area with thick underbrush. Preferably one surrounded by mature forest. It depends upon tornados or fire or loggers to disturb a large enough chunk of forest. One it can nest in." In my excitement, I missed the obvious irony I'd created. My students didn't.

"You mean it needs a clear-cut?" Brianna asked innocently, scribbling in her field notebook.

"Um . . . well . . . in a way, yes," I responded.

"So a clear-cut is good?" she pressed, her pen poised like a hummingbird inspecting a flower.

Several students began taking notes. I paused again, knowing poor word choice would erode what little remained of my credibility.

"It's ultimately a question about values. Or tradeoffs, for that matter. Should we eliminate habitat for a goshawk to create it for the warbler? Or rather, exclude the warbler for the goshawk? What do you all think?" I asked. Although new at teaching, I'd quickly learned the quasi-duplicitous art of asking a question to stall for time. Time I needed to sort out my own values. "We'll discuss this more after lunch," I said, knowing my lunchtime would be spent boning up on avian habitat preferences. "We need to get back."

Since my students knew the route back to the vans, I intentionally took the rear. I needed to avoid conversation, time to think. Yet again, I had stumbled into one of my many limitations. I held an advanced degree in ecology that didn't seem to help me much. As I learned with the tanager and thrush, ecology, like many other disciplines, frequently breeched the walls of others, like philosophy.

It's one thing to understand habitat preferences of goshawks and warblers; it's another to blend it with an organized system of values, or ethics. The goshawk and warbler both share a right to exist and thrive. As do the great-horned owls, woodcocks, red-backed salamanders, and countless other organisms making up this patch. The hunter feels a right to his deer and we all want timber and paper products. How do we organize these values? Even harder, how do we rank them? No wonder the application of all these values—conservation biology—is so difficult to do well. All of it requires firm ecological footing, local indigenous knowledge, equitable stakeholder involvement, and a touch of teleology. This is why the most honest conservation biology textbooks begin with several chapters devoted solely to the valuation of species. Conservation is an applied science with a mission: the long-term survival of all species. To do it well, one can't hole up in an ivory tower.

I often revel in such transdisciplinary endeavors. Difficult, sure. But immensely relevant.

And risky. Expertise, I knew from experience, only goes so far. So when I do storm another colleague's castle? And how should I do it? How far can—or should—I go? So much, I'm learning, rides on this question: the academic lives of my students, their future professions and choices, and the invaluable lives of goshawks and warblers, among myriad other creatures.

By the time we piled in the vans, I hadn't come any closer to answering the goshawk-versus-warbler question. Nor the question about how and when to log forests. The answers are undeniably complex. I had arrived at a simpler truth, previously obscured by the tangle of questions: when I'm teaching—or preaching—about the philosophy of nature, humility must be lesson number one. As the mourning warbler reminded me with its clarion call, answers to nature's most important questions are rarely clear-cut.

20 · DUTCH BLITZ BIRDING

Never do anything by halves if you want to get away with it. Be outrageous. Go the whole hog. Make sure everything you do is so completely crazy it's unbelievable.

—Roald Dahl, *Matilda*

"Dad? Dad? Where are you going?" Ezra asked, glancing up from a thick book he was reading, titled *Bomb*.

"No time to explain!" I grabbed my binoculars and covered the living room in three determined strides. The speed of my movement caught the attention of Indigo and Willow, who shared Ezra's curiosity.

"No, Dad, seriously. What is it?" he pressed.

"Varied thrush," I replied, opening the screen door and letting it slam behind me.

"I'm coming." Ezra snapped *Bomb* closed and leapt off the couch like a startled housecat. My terse explanation had detonated something inside him. Unlike his younger sisters, Ezra was accustomed to such moments, moments when I flouted familial norms for the sake of a bird. I rarely pulled such explanation-less stunts with houseguests and friends. I'd embarrassed myself so many times with my family, however, that there was no reason to rein it in.

"Where did you see it?" Ezra asked, joining me in the backyard. Sensing my urgency, he hadn't bothered with a coat despite the brisk October weather.

"Just here, about thirty seconds ago." I scanned the shrubbery.

"Have you seen one before?" he asked, more interested in my life list than I often was.

"Yeah," I replied. "But never well . . . and never in the yard. This one must be a migrant."

So focused in the search, I didn't notice our neighbor, Melanie, until she greeted us. "What are you guys doing?" She restrained her leashed dog while staring at my binoculars. I turned red. Here I was, stalking through the bushes a stone's throw from her house. Her question—and latent suspicion—was justified.

"Oh, hi, Melanie," I replied. "We, uh, saw a cool bird and . . ."

"Actually, my dad saw a varied thrush." Ezra felt none of my hesitancy. "My dad has already seen one, but I need to see it for my life list."

"I wish my father had shown me birds when I was little," Melanie said wishfully, allowing her dog to pull her away. Her well-chosen words erased my sheepishness, and I resumed searching for the thrush. We canvassed the yard. There it was, out front, uncharacteristically in the open. Like all my previous experiences with this retiring bird, the thrush immediately flew up into an evergreen and dissolved into the dark green foliage.

"That's a good find," I said to Ezra as we headed for the house. "I've never seen one out in the open before. It must have momentarily mistaken itself for a robin."

When it comes to welcoming others into my nature-loving proclivities, I've long been a secretive varied thrush. My inner robin emerges only when it has to, when I'm teaching or with my kids. These shy tendencies started early. I've pointed out white-crowned sparrows to the wrong crowd before. Snickers and sarcasm, even done with love, taught me not to repeat my mistake. I learned to be judicious, acknowledging my interests only to a few trusted, equally interested folks.

My interest, it seemed, wasn't cool-fringe. Rather, it was weird-fringe, something I'd hopefully grow out of. Without much validation from family or friends, I buried my interest as deeply as I could. I even hoped to outgrow it. Stubbornly, it remained perched. Steadfast. Determined to one day fledge, my interest soon moved to the edge of the nest and began testing its wings.

In high school, this sometimes proved inconvenient. While my ultra-cool friends drove around listening to Smashing Pumpkins and Pearl Jam, I secretly opted for backyard birdsong cassettes, stashing them well under my seat when others rode along. Later on, in college, I hung my small waste bin outside my window and loaded it with oranges I nicked from the cafeteria. All so I could watch northern orioles as I hammered out tedious research papers on my dryer-sized computer (my roommate, who once consumed an entire jar of mayonnaise in one sitting, was quirky enough not to question it).

Whether it was a slowly growing self-confidence or merely an uncharacteristic lapse, I'll never know, but the day my robin burst forth remains indelibly etched. Entirely coincidentally, the moment also involved a varied thrush.

We had just concluded an intense week of outdoor education, leading groups of fifth graders through the redwood forests of central California. Per usual, we were sitting in a semicircle on the floor of our collective office, recounting the week before disbanding for the weekend. Our director, Scott, read through the week's generally positive evaluations as we soaked in the satisfaction that comes with a grueling week of work.

Mentally drained, I allowed my unfocused gaze to wander to the large bay window directly over Scott's head. Outside was a curtain of green, boughs of bigleaf maple intertwined with endless sprays of conifer needles. Suddenly an actor robed in apricot orange dropped onto the shimmering green stage. His eye-catching garb included a large ebony necklace.

"Varied thrush!" The words tumbled out before I could stop them. Everybody looked where I pointed. Scott put his papers on the floor and turned to look as well. I bit my lip and cringed, realizing I'd rudely interrupted him.

The thrush cocked its head twice as if feeling suddenly overdressed compared to our motley earth tone apparel. It disappeared as quickly as it had come, back into the forest's gloom. Scott turned back around and picked up his papers. As with Melanie, his appreciative smile killed all the regret and embarrassment I'd felt.

"That," Scott said matter-of-factly, "is a cool bird."

After our meeting, Scott pulled me aside. "Eli," he said, "I called the local bird hotline this morning. A Sprague's pipit is hanging out down around Elkhorn Slough. I'm going after it. Might play some soccer on the way home with some friends. Wanna come?"

At the time, I had no idea what a bird hotline was. Nor what a Sprague's pipit looked like. I didn't even know that otherwise sane people got in cars and drove to chase birds. But I knew one thing. I was going with Scott.

Scott, I soon deduced, was a robin. He had no qualms about who he was and what he liked. I had played my hand by pointing out the varied thrush. Sensing a willing partner, he had offered to teach me a new game, bird chasing. It was complex, involved strategy, and offered lots of unforeseen reward. I was hooked. With one simple invitation to chase a Sprague's pipit, my game of Solitaire—keep-it-to-myself, self-conscious birding—morphed into rambunctious, multi-player Dutch Blitz.

My confidence in the validity of my interests has grown a

lot since the varied thrush perched picturesquely outside my employer's window. Birding, too, has changed. After languishing for decades as a trifling tributary, it's now a mainstream hobby, even a sport. While defining a birder is tough, the Fish and Wildlife Service claimed at one point that the United States boasted forty-seven million birders. Most of these—forty-one million—were the well-adjusted species that stays at home. I'd call them birdwatchers. This means that six million Americans follow birds on the road, travelling, as the report said, at least one mile away from home. Not bad. If a quorum represents a minimum number of people to make something valid, then I'd say a quorum we have.

A hobby, in my case, led to a profession. When I landed a professorship, it included teaching an ornithology course. And other courses, like conservation biology and wildlife behavior, in which birds could be incorporated with ease. Finally, it seemed, I needn't justify my tendency to let my gaze drift skyward. Despite all this progression, I've realized a varied thrush doesn't molt all at once; it loses just a few feathers at a time. My tendency to retire back into the forest's gloom continues to occur with unsettling regularity.

A few weeks ago, I headed into the foothills of southern Oregon to look for a bird I'd long wanted to see: a white-headed woodpecker. The avian gods smiled that gorgeous fall evening, as I hobnobbed with an obliging pair of the very woodpeckers I'd sought as they shimmied up ponderosa pine trees. Their pure white heads seemed to shimmer in the sun as they pried up loose bark. It seemed the pair was renovating rotten shingles from their summer cottage.

The sun soon dipped below the horizon, sending the woodpeckers off in search of a roost. I headed back down the way I'd come, found a trail, and soon bumped into two of my students, Tyler and Connor. These two were not in an ornithology course, however, and I'd yet to let them in on my interests.

"Great sunset!" I said with a wide smile, attempting to throw them off of the real reason I had trekked uphill. Because old habits die hard, my cheeks turned red as embarrassment flooded over me. I felt guilty, like I'd been caught licking the innards of a jelly packet at a breakfast diner. I didn't want to admit that a little-known species had pulled me there with black hole-like force.

Again, my binoculars betrayed me. Both students stared at them dangling like a bullseye around my neck. People don't watch sunsets with binoculars. I was busted red-handed. I had to come clean.

"Found a really cool bird," I admitted, waiting for the usual smirks and sarcasm that had scarred my childhood. Eyebrows went up, but my students' faces revealed little. "White-headed woodpeckers," I went on, my enthusiasm slowly waxing. "They're thinly distributed, so I got really lucky. It's the only woodpecker with a completely white head, and they..." I stopped myself. Though I was over my initial embarrassment, it occurred to me that this kind of over-the-top zeal might confirm what I suspected they were thinking: that I was a bona fide kook.

Tyler and Connor nodded, patiently listening as I explained what I found most fascinating about the birds. When I finished, Tyler thrust his hands in his pockets and said something entirely unexpected. "When are we going to get to go birding?" He was earnest. Such mutual interest was even better than the birds themselves.

Some moments, however, lack such redemption. Several years ago, I led an ornithology trip in Wells State Park, in Massachusetts. While the students were setting up their tents, I wandered down a trail and noticed some flowers of lowbush blueberry in full bloom. They were exquisite. I dropped down on all fours to better see the delicate bell-shaped flowers. They hung from the thin branches like miniature Christmas ornaments. The slanting sun's rays transformed the petals into petticoats, and I pulled out my camera to catch the fleeting moment. For the most dramatic angle, I had to point my camera upward. I rolled over onto my back. Utterly immersed in the ephemeral still life, I failed to notice a pair of backpackers who broke my trance with a simple question. "Whatcha lookin' at?" the man in front asked, looking down at me with the intensity of a half-time football coach.

Startled, I sat up, my cheeks flooding with color. This time, it wasn't about birds. But marble-sized blueberry blossoms felt equally insignificant. "I . . . uh . . . well, nothing, really." I stood up and shoved my camera in my bag. A woman stood behind her inquisitive hiking partner. A black ponytail stuck out of a blue bandana covering her head. She peeked warily around the man, conveying none of his curiosity.

The couple sensed my reluctance and didn't press me for more. I sidestepped the trail, casting my eyes downward as they marched on by. "Have a good evening," I called after them, already regretting the entire exchange. I knew what they had to be thinking: just another weirdo hanging out in the woods. They'd likely sleep with one eye open tonight.

My regret, revealed by retrospect, is less about embarrassment and more about missed opportunity. Caught with my hand in the cookie jar doing something I love, I've found that I'm prone to prevaricate, skirting the truth in hapless attempts to save face. I most certainly was looking at something along the trail in Wells State Park: a Lilliputian wonder, alabaster blueberry blossoms so marvelously backlit that they looked like ghostly processions ascending from the earth. Because they hung just inches from the ground, I had walked by hundreds before noticing them. It was obvious the backpacking pair had missed them too. But because my confidence had faltered, I missed an opportunity to share the spectacle.

Our world is jam-packed with spectacle and wonders. Some of them, from stunning sunsets to granite peaks, are so obvious that everybody sees them. Others, like white-headed woodpeckers and blueberry blossoms, are surreptitious and subtle, harder to see but equally worthy of attention. Another juniper titmouse. I've come to realize the opportunity to share nature's finer touches with interested people doesn't come every day. So when it does, I should shuck my vestigial embarrassment like an ear of corn.

While it's fine for the thrush to sing from the forest gloom, my song is better served when it's heard in the open, robin-like. It's good to march out of the house seeking an exquisitely hued varied thrush. Even better when my son follows me out. Or when my students ask to tag along. Occasionally, it's even okay to interrupt a meeting to point a thrush out. Why? Because my response to those who are earnestly seeking nature's overlooked wonders shouldn't be varied at all.

Part III

CHICKEN SOUP FOR AN OUTDOOR-LOVER'S SOUL

21 · Flying Through the Bird Portal

The diversity of life forms, so numerous that we have yet to identify most of them, is the greatest wonder on this planet.

—E. O. Wilson

The solitary man on the deserted beach was obviously not looking for company. He was staring through binoculars at a bunch of floating specks bobbing up and down on overcast Lake Michigan. Drips of water rolled off the back of his full-brimmed hat, soaking into his oversized, many-pocketed vest.

I wasn't looking for company either. But something about this guy intrigued me; his very indifference drew me in. I sidled up about ten feet away and pretended to look through my own fogged-up binoculars. I waited for an opening. After another minute, he lowered his binoculars but continued staring straight ahead.

"Seen any Nelson's lately?" I asked, sneaking a sideways glance. My question was pointed and strategic. To the general public, it was overtly nonsensical. Even to many birders, it was cryptic. But if I had judged correctly, my four-word question would form a bond, and potentially open up a portal. A portal that could shed light on the birds of Chicago, of which I knew little.

"I don't look at 'em." He shrugged his shoulders, still avoiding eye contact. His terse response reaffirmed my hunch that this guy was content with his own company. It also affirmed that we were speaking the same language. A code. Birder trade talk. He knew what a Nelson's was. That's why I found his answer baffling. Why didn't he look at sparrows? If he was studying a raft of faraway ducks, he was being disingenuous. He looked and spoke like a serious birder. But what serious birder ignores sparrows? Especially uncommon, migrant sparrows? Sparrows, I'd learned in my birding forays with others, separate the wheat from the chaff. If you know your sparrows, you're legit. If you don't, well, you better learn them. If you want to be taken seriously by the birding crowd, that is.

So although this laconic misanthropist wanted to be left alone, I was too curious to grant him his wish. I pretended to look through my binoculars again as I sought out my next line. Oddly, I didn't have to. Sensing my stubborn curiosity, he spoke. "I look at shorebirds." He lifted the bottom of his vest to wipe the eyepieces of his binoculars. He fell silent again. I opted for silence myself, hoping he'd say more. It worked. "There are some sparrows about three miles from here that you should sift through. I didn't bother." With that, he stole a quick glance at me and raised his binoculars again. Was he done? I needed a little bit more.

With binoculars raised, I told him I was a New Yorker and had only an hour here at Montrose Point, one of Chicago's key migrant traps. He nodded approval, and then, ever so methodically, gave me some of the most explicit directions I've ever received. The kind of directions that made me know he wanted me to find what I was looking for. "Best of luck," he said, extending his hand. I had a dozen more questions I wanted to ask. I willed myself not to. He had allowed me access to a portal of privileged information. For this, I would return him his solitude. I sincerely thanked him and turned on my heels.

Optimistic about finding a new bird with my precious new info, I walked briskly to my car. Anxious as I was to look for a Nelson's sparrow, I couldn't shake my newfound confusion. A few things were certain. The shorebird man and I were both birders. Both of us were likely utilizing small windows of time to pursue particular species. But there was a key difference, too. He was a bona fide specialist studying shorebirds. He wasn't bothering with other species. I, however, was a consummate generalist. Granted, I was currently pursuing a Nelson's sparrow. But most of the time, I wasn't. I was easily distractible. If I stumbled into a milk snake, a pretty orb-weaving spider, or even just a really interesting person, I could—and would—be redirected instantly. My priority list simply pushed me outside. I wasn't exclusive; the "I don't look at 'em" shorebird man was. Which approach was better?

My all-inclusive mission started well before I was listening to bird cassettes and hanging waste bins out my dorm room window. First it was deer. I watched them. Stalked them. And counted them obsessively. Then one summer, I noticed a chestnut-sided warbler singing from a power line stretched across a blackberry thicket. The yellow crown and the neat little streak of chestnut running down the flanks made the bird look carefully hand-painted. It was the spark that set off an inferno. I was soon scanning treetops and shorelines everywhere I went.

Deer and birds were just the starting point. Soon I was noticing—and trying to name—trees, butterflies, beetles, and flowers. It mushroomed to include even mushrooms. I realized how wide my interests ranged when a healthy dose of last-minute restraint was all that prevented me from purchasing Winter Weed Finder: A Guide to Dry Plants in Winter. No, I wasn't searching out hidden marijuana plots. Nor do I know why I wanted—and still like to—identify weeds in winter. I likely never will. But I do know it has something to do with wanting to untangle the web of creation I'm firmly woven into.

At Montrose Point, all I knew about Nelson's sharp-tailed sparrows was that they existed. And thanks to the Internet and the tattered field guide sliding around the floor of my rental car, I knew they passed through Illinois on migration. But if I found the bird and watched it for a while, my understanding would molt like the sparrow, head knowledge would be supplanted by the richer, deeper humus of experience. I'd arrive at that critical portal; a portal that, once passed through, begets a relationship.

That's why despite my confusion, I felt affection for the shorebird man. Regardless of his desires, he had made himself a portal giving me a chance to kick-start a relationship with another species. What he hadn't told me, however, was how bad traffic would be in those three measly miles. Not more than a mile down the road, things came to a standstill. A standstill paralleling my present predicament in taxonomy.

I have always loved naming nature. Had the Lord given me Adam's task in the garden to name every creature, humankind would not be fallen. Instead of being seduced by the serpent, I would have spent my time discerning whether its pupils were round or elliptical. Too preoccupied with keying out the tree of good and evil, I wouldn't have bothered eating the forbidden fruit. Wherever I am and wherever I go, I affix genus-species names to everything I see. The way some people can't bring themselves to step on a sidewalk crack, I am beholden to naming nature. Lately, in the past few years, I've become overwhelmed. Not by the few names I know, but by the endless ones I don't.

On my best days, I confidently call myself a naturalist and saunter out for an ego-assuaging woodland stroll. I level my gaze, identify oaks and daisies, and avert my eyes from anything smaller. On my worst days—most days—I amble out, accidentally drop my gaze by my doorstep, and feel mocked by a mushroom that is different than the others. Before I manage to reach the woods, I notice a fern. Could it be a New York fern? Or is it cinnamon? Perhaps elegant fern? A breeze blows. Zipping up my fleece, I notice a beetle has chosen me for its preferred mode of public transport. Coleoptera, I mumble, merely assigning it an order that includes almost half a million described species. That's all I can do with most beetles. No family. No genus. And certainly no species. I return home an hour later, tail between my legs, soaked anew in my estrangement from my natural neighbors and my abject failure as a naturalist. This, I've realized, is my clear and present taxonomic predicament. It is also the curse of the nature-loving generalist.

Slowly but surely this curse bequeathed me a most unwelcome gift—an inferiority complex. The complex metastasized and soon became chronic and debilitating. Several years ago, I resolved to end it. I armed myself with field guides to everything and went outside. My motto was simple: one species per stroll. Joe-pye weed on Tuesday, shaggy mane on Wednesday, chickweed on Thursday, and on it went. Steadfast in my pursuit, I kept it up, every day that I could. The strategy served me well.

But lately in this process, I've caught a whiff of my mortality. The wires of my recognition powers have frayed, some coming loose altogether. And my memory seems saturated. I've plateaued to a point that biogeographers would gleefully refer to as a dynamic equilibrium. For every new species that colonizes my mind, another grows hazy and blinks out. The long view is obvious. It's also bleak. Even if I forsake my family and dedicate all my remaining days to my taxonomic quest, I will fall woefully short. My epitaph is as clear as Scrooge's, and for me at least, equally foreboding: here lies a man who barely scratched the surface. Human classification abilities are just that limited. Or, rather, nature is just that grand.

It wouldn't be so bad if nature identification was one of my hobbies. But it's not; it's part of my profession. As a professor of several biology courses, I'm supposed to teach this stuff. Each and every year, I teach courses to students who have unloaded their bank accounts to receive knowledge I've accrued. I'm the professor; it's my job to profess about theories and principles and relationships. Without species recognition in basic field courses, it's hard to profess about anything. With or without a hand lens, there are a lot of critters out there. Somewhere in the ballpark of 100,000,000 million. And the more I learn, the more I realize I don't know, even here in the benign and relatively depauperate northeastern United States. Herein is a problem. And herein is the genius of the shorebird man—the specialist—that I met on Montrose Point in Chicago.

If there's any comfort for my quandary it's that others, far more luminary than myself, have been mired in it too. It's easy to deduce from the journals Charles Darwin kept while on board the Beagle that he was interested in everything. Iguanas, finches, fossils, plants. He amassed a mountain of observations. Like me, he tried to name what he could. Despite even Darwin's taxonomic prowess, he was gun shy with his theory of evolution. He felt he knew everything and nothing. So he hit the pause button—for eight years—and willed himself to become a specialist. His choice? Barnacles.

After seeing wonder upon wonder and doing experiments with far more compelling creatures, some find it flabbergasting that Darwin chose barnacles as his specialty. But I think I know why. He wanted to know something few others did. He was tired of being a generalist. He craved depth and the confidence it often bestows. Barnacles, insipid and mind numbing as they appear to the unmotivated, offered just that.

Many of the great naturalists were consummate generalists.

They knew a lot about a lot. But when they were collecting specimens, the world was smaller. Travel was slower and harder. Many naturalists studied what they could around home. After returning from his five-year Beagle voyage, for example, Darwin clung to England with the steadfastness of the barnacles he pored over. Others never took a voyage at all. Remaining home in the temperate latitudes—where fewer species lived—made gaining competence in the natural world far easier.

Today, however, we're saturated in information. If I'm confident in my yard, an entirely different ecosystem—a bog or a meadow—is a short drive down the road. And if I get those amazingly complex systems down, entirely different biomes are half-day flights away. Not long ago, it took people months to arrive in Africa from the states. Today it's just a day or two.

Like Darwin, Harvard naturalist E. O. Wilson realized how overwhelming the natural world is. Perhaps that's why he started as a generalist but soon specialized in Phediole ants, one genus among the hundreds comprising the Formicidae family. Life is too short and the tree of life too vast to ever master the myriad branches. One tiny twig is all we can hope for.

Perhaps that's why the shorebird man from Montrose Point didn't look at sparrows. Shorebirds, in their ever-changing plumages and abundance, are exceedingly difficult to identify. Their behavior and multifaceted life histories are just as complicated. Field guide makers have realized this and devoted entire books to this group of birds alone. Perhaps the shorebird man was following advice offered by the late technology guru, Steve Jobs. "Do not try to do everything," Jobs quipped. "Do one thing well."

I desperately want to do one thing well, too. With every year that passes, I wonder if this ability simply isn't enmeshed in my double helix strands. I'm interested in too much, too much in awe of nature to only admire its leading actors. I want to know the extras, the costume producers, camera crew, even the caterers. Doing one thing well or many things poorly is a conundrum that, unlike Darwin, I'm not sure I have any control over. Darwin was a curious polymath but had an added ability to ignore what wasn't right in front of him. He finished what he started. That's how he mastered barnacles. It was this rare combination of gifts that made him the ultimate portal through which millions have passed. His ability to generalize, specialize, and then generalize again has given us all a better understanding of the tree of life, and ultimately, why it's so crucial to conserve it.

For better or worse, I lack both Darwin's abilities and his drive. This doesn't excuse me from being a portal. The rivets on the plane are falling out too fast; biodiversity is plummeting too quickly for any of us to forsake opening up the natural world for others. All of us, specialists and generalists alike, need to be portals for those who can't—or won't—find the wonders of nature any other way.

Despite the shorebird man's explicit directions, darkness settled too quickly and cars moved too slowly for me to find a Nelson's sparrow that evening. But the next day, my last in Chicago, I found myself again with a few more hours before nightfall. Time wouldn't allow a trip back to the sparrows near Montrose Point. I pulled out my maps and settled for Springbrook Prairie, a small preserve with an equally small marsh, in DuPage County. Used to exploring large tracts, I expected little from the preserve that is hemmed in on all sides by well-trafficked streets. There was no way I'd find a Nelson's here. I nixed it from my target list, relaxed, and let my inner generalist run wild. Run it did.

Right away I noticed two northern harriers performing their choppy, bat-like flight over the senescing meadow grass. Peaceful minutes passed as I watched them patrol the prairie waiting to pounce on unwary rabbits. Two blue-winged teal exploded off the marsh, nearly stopping my heart in the process. I ambled under lavender skies, threading my fingers through purple-colored asters. Nearing the end of my soul-renewing jaunt, I noticed several sparrows perched atop some cattails. Ever hopeful, I raised my binoculars. Right away my pulse steadied. They were all Savannah sparrows, every last one of them. They flew off, disappearing into the gloaming.

I let my gaze linger, thinking I saw another teal snaking through the cattails. Whatever I thought I saw eluded me. But my search was not in vain. Another small shape caught my eye, deep within the cattail stems: a sparrow with a slightly different gestalt. I studied it in the twilight, noting the placement of each streak and shade. Yes indeed. Right there, just ten yards away, settling down to spend this crisp September night, was a little Nelson's sharp-tailed sparrow.

I knew this sparrow. Mostly because I had prepared for it. Despite this success, I'll never have all the sparrows mastered. Nor all the shorebirds. Not even all the species in my three-acre yard. I'll haplessly keep trying, of course, but will fall woefully short. I love all of nature too much to focus for too long on any one part.

There's a twist, however. Just because I'm a generalist doesn't mean I can't do one thing well. The one thing I can do well, as the shorebird man showed me, is showing others what they need: nature. For sanity amidst life's chaos. For rejuvenation amidst life's busyness. And for peace amidst life's upheaval. I can be a portal. Without one, most people will never behold harriers hunting over a marsh. Or have their hearts stopped by blue-winged teal. And they'll certainly never savor a species unlikely to ever merit a headline until it's extinct. Small, yes. But still worth seeing. An unassuming sparrow crouched down in the cattails.

22 · MY CHICKADEE EPIPHANY

I will be standing in the woods
where the old trees
move only with the wind
and then with gravity.

—Wendell Berry, *Stay Home*

Life depends on death. Every single molecule of it. I know this now. I did not know it when I was a high school senior on a weeklong camping trip just before my first day of college. At eighteen years old, I took great joy in my vitality. One of the inexplicable ways I celebrated this joy was by searching out dead—but still standing—trees in the forest and then pushing them over like an overwrought Neanderthal. Some trees required little more than a gentle nudge. Others—the ones I liked best—required me to lower my shoulder, run, and then ram. The resulting crash was as satisfying as the initial smash. My backpacking comrades smiled weakly each time I darted after a deceased tree. They humored me, cringing with every crash. But they didn't stop me. Oh, how I wish they had.

Now, many years later and armed with an in-depth ecological education, these memories make *me* cringe. While my environmental sins are without excuse, they were born of ignorance, not malice. And I'm guessing that my hiking friends at the time were equally ignorant; hence their collective ambivalence.

Most bad habits endure a protracted struggle before they die. Not my tree tipping. It died instantly. It was a breezy June morning and I was birding at the end of a forested road. A black-capped chickadee glided by and perched atop a broken-off, decaying tree. Its diameter was slightly smaller than a telephone pole, the tree resembling more of a tall stump. Just the kind of thing I loved to topple. I stared at the chickadee, mesmerized by its ability to scold my presence without losing the wiggling green caterpillar in its bill. The bird hopped onto a low hemlock, bashed the caterpillar on a branch, scolded me again, and flew back to the stump. Then, like Frodo slipping on the ring, it vanished. Poof.

I blinked. How had *that* happened? Had I discovered a rare species of vaporizing chickadee? I scrambled to the broken-off tree, shimmied up the wobbly trunk, and peered down in.

HISS! I yanked my head out. Whoa. Was there a snake in there? Possibly. Ever so gently, I peeked back in. The hissing started anew. This time, I willed myself to remain. My eyes gradually adjusted to the dimly lit interior. About three feet down was the chickadee. Its bill was empty. Shockingly, the little irate bird puffed itself up and hissed at me like a rankled rat snake. Underneath it were three fuzzy heads. They seemed as befuddled as me. Unable to maintain my awkward position any longer, I slid down the tree and regained my feet. Now I understood why Tom Brown Jr., in his timeless classic, *The Tracker*, proclaimed the chickadee greater than the owl, the crow, and the jay. Here indeed was a bird with an indomitable spirit.

I ran my hand along the tree's flaky, lichen-encrusted bark. With my fingernails, I could dig into the rotten remains. This tree wasn't just dead. It was long dead. Yet inside its hollowed-out heart, new life was unfurling. This tree no longer provided shade and oxygen like its fellow forest compatriots. Yet here it stood, stubbornly determined to bestow as many parting gifts as possible. For the three helpless chicks inside, this gift was more important than all the others offered by the larger leafy giants. This tree had been selected carefully. Its spongy walls had allowed the parents to excavate a chamber that living trees could not provide. Chickadees don't have the built-in jackhammer bills that woodpeckers do. Nor do they have all the adaptive head-banging headgear. Their weak, multi-purpose bills need soft, rotten wood. Flimsy, yes. But without the protective spongy walls the tree provided, the chickadee chicks would hardly last an hour in the forest. Their lives had depended on the death of this tree. Now they depended on the death of countless invertebrates if they were to fledge in the coming weeks.

This tenuous tree would stand. As would all dead and dying trees from this point thereafter. It was a small but searing epiphany. I shoved my hands in my pockets and wandered away, wondering what other ecological sins I'd committed in my youth.

John Burroughs was right when he said there is news in every bush. I had always assumed he meant living bushes. The truth, I realized, extended well beyond green vegetation. Nature, as Aristotle famously penned, abhors a vacuum. Niches become filled. Resources get used. Everything eventually provides for something else. True, the tree no longer offered fodder for deer and rabbits nor shade for songbirds. Yet it kept on giving what it could: a hotel for beetles, a buffet for woodpeckers, and as I'd discovered, shelter for chickadees. In due time, when it gave way to gravity, it'd provide the same for red-backed salamanders and saprophytes, not to mention all the nutrients it'd return to the soil. "There is no death," Chief Seattle once said, "only a change in worlds."

The deeper I've dug into death, the more life-giving it seems.

Living organisms, like us, are composed of cells and tissues. These are made of complex organic molecules, called macromolecules. Macromolecules, like triglyceride fats in animal cells or cellulose in plants, are maintained and added by organisms and the cells within them. By their very nature, living beings and their tissues counteract decomposition. Maintenance and growth functions defy death. When death does come, however, like the caterpillar bashed by the chickadee, maintenance and growth functions cease. Had the caterpillar corpse been lost on the forest floor (and miraculously not eaten), decomposition would have taken over. Living tissue and cells would have broken down. The caterpillar's macromolecules would have broken down into simpler organic and inorganic molecules. We habitually thank the Lord for our daily bread. We should thank Him for decomposition, too. Without it, there'd be a lot of dead caterpillars underfoot. And dead everything, for that matter. Forget climbing Everest. The endless mountainous piles of dead biomass would be far more challenging.

The taproot of this awakening has penetrated my soul. The emerging cotyledons are now affecting my approach as well. Whenever friends or relatives ask me to help remove the ugly dead stuff from their lawns, I bristle. I hem and haw and search for an excuse. When Linda asks me to lop off a dead limb, I get uneasy. Sweat forms on my forehead. I mumble things. Others have shared my reluctance. Even those in high places. When the White House was being remodeled during Teddy Roosevelt's presidency, his wife, Edith, refused to allow the removal of seventy bushes from the terrace. She refused despite being promised the bushes would be carefully removed and replanted in New Jersey. No way. It was either her or the bushes. While Edith's true motivations are unknown, I like to think that she too, had a chickadee epiphany. Or, that her refusal was an atonement for a former life of ignorant tree tipping.

Too many people believe that dead trees must be removed to allow for beautiful lawns and landscapes. Since my conversion, however, dead trees create beautiful landscapes. I'm fine being in the minority. Dead trees are worth it. They're harbingers for the many other creatures I love to share my space with. They're buffet tables, lookouts, and condominiums. As long as they're not posing a hazard, the dead trees in my yard will remain upright. I know they'll one day topple. But I'll concede this timetable to nature. I don't want more blood on my hands than I already have. Every night the chickadee settles over its helpless young in its weak-walled—but sufficient—abode, it is reminded anew. As I am now. That life, every single molecule of it, depends on death.

23 · Life's Harrier Moments

*When you look at the dark side, careful you must be.
For the dark side looks back.*

—Yoda

L ife comes with no guarantees. Despite our greatest efforts to plan and prepare, curveballs come when we least expect it. Ultimately, even the strongest of our species—the richest and most powerful—are one literal stroke away from their own demise. Be it car crash or cancer, seizure or tsunami, we are all united by our vulnerability.

As a father of three under ten, I feel this more deeply than most. Like many things I can't control, I am loath to dwell on it. Fortunately, this was a rare day I didn't have to; Linda had volunteered to juggle the daily routine of the kids: friend's houses, meal preps, and constant diaper management. Take a day, she generously suggested, to reclaim peace and quiet. I wouldn't argue with that. But where could I find such a place devoid of people yet abounding in beauty? After a few minutes poring over an outdated road atlas, I settled on a remote meadow in the middle of Pennsylvania.

It wasn't just any old meadow. It had sprung from the wreckage of a mining site. Native flowers and grasses had reclaimed the land and with them, the butterflies and birds. Bathed anew in native biodiversity, the meadows were eventually protected as state game lands. To most, these featureless fields are nothing more than "reclaimed mines," and largely ignored. But I know better. They're magical. Partly because they're devoid of my own species yet surfeit with others, namely sparrows. No, the mysterious shorebird man of Montrose Point certainly wouldn't be here.

In addition to seeking silence, I sought sparrows. Approximately nine different sparrow species called the mines home in the summer—some of them rare and highly sought after. I'd seek them out, wander, relax, and return home revitalized.

At first, everything proceeded apace. I parked my car, sat down in the middle of a meadow, and gazed at a grasshopper sparrow about a school bus's length away. Perched atop a teasel twig, it held a freshly nabbed, writhing caterpillar in its bill. Put off by my presence, the sparrow flicked its tail, feverishly admonishing me. It was obvious why this sparrow wasn't swallowing its snack. It was early June. Undoubtedly, a ravenous rabble of hungry nestlings waited impatiently nearby.

Miraculously, after carefully following the sparrow's flight path, I soon found the nest. And as I suspected, it harbored four, pink, helpless inhabitants. It was hard to believe that despite being the size of a strawberry, each little nestling was packed with elaborate double helices of DNA. With little more than a steady diet of arthropods, these blueprints would allow them in just weeks to fly and sing and fend for themselves. But for now at least, they were vulnerability epitomized.

Thankful for my lofty position at the top of the food chain and awakened anew to life's fragility, I retraced my steps to the dirt road that bisected the meadow. That's when I saw the harrier. It sat atop a stout shrub of honeysuckle, the only available perch anywhere in sight. It was white and gray, a male. How close, I wondered, would this superior prairie predator let me approach?

I left the road and walked an intentional wide arc around

the harrier, slowly cutting the distance to the bird. The harrier saw right through my flimsy façade. With a few powerful strokes, it launched off the honeysuckle and came after me like a heat-seeking missile. With a high-pitched *KEK-KEK-KEK-KEK*, the shrieking harrier locked its yellow eyes on my own.

There was nowhere to hide. I glanced in the direction of my car and scrambled toward it backwards, unwilling to lose track of the belligerent bird. The harrier had full advantage and came within feet of my face, unfolding its talons as it passed. Like the sparrow, this bird obviously had vulnerable young nearby.

Thankfully, my feet found the dirt road. Its ire raised, the unrelenting harrier continued its series of swoops, giving me an angry airborne escort all the way to my car. I fumbled the door open and fell into the driver's seat. Only then did I exhale.

Satisfied by my retreat, the harrier returned to its perch to resume its parental duties. I glanced at my watch and knew it was time to resume duties of my own.

The wildflower meadows slowly disappeared in my rearview mirror as I started back for home. As hoped, I was meditative and at peace. In just a few hours, I had seen the multiple faces of vulnerability. I had always dwelt on its downside. Now I realized it had an upside, too. Like nothing else, vulnerability had placed me in the present moment. My minutes with the sparrow and the harrier blocked everything else out. It felt good. It felt rejuvenating. Rather than rue my children's vulnerability, I was now ready to embrace it. With nothing guaranteed, I would enjoy them while I could. Perhaps this newfound outlook would allow me, like the meadows, to be reclaimed.

24 · BIRDFEEDER BLUES

We shall never achieve harmony with land, any more than we shall achieve absolute justice or liberty for people. In these higher aspirations, the important thing is not to achieve but to try.

—Aldo Leopold

Last fall, I became yet another victim of a hungry bear. The fateful morning is indelibly etched in my mind. I awoke to bright sunshine and, as I do every morning, ambled over to our big picture windows to quickly ascertain the basic facts that support my existence. The trees were upright. The grass still needed mowing. And neglected toys lay scattered about like shrapnel. Yes, everything seemed in order. Or was it?

What was that odd lump of dirty plastic doing there? And what were those plastic shards strewn about? Hey, who stole the birdfeeder? Too alarmed and annoyed to don shoes, I stormed outside to more closely examine the lump of plastic and Plexiglas that was formerly a feeder. It was mangled. Shattered, broken, punctured, and scratched. It looked as if a small meteorite had fallen in the night and hit it while missing all else. Like a bin of Legos had been dumped upon the floor. More pitiful was the pathetic party of chickadees and juncos that hopped amidst the wreckage just feet from my own, looking for seed that survived the impact.

Although unskilled in forensics, the claw marks, mud smears, and teeth-sized puncture holes all pointed to one perpetrator, hirsute and ursine. Further investigations revealed a chewed-up suet holder one hundred yards from its original location and some suspicious piles of scat. I walked back inside, wet socks and all, and for the first time in my life, began begrudging bears.

But time, as the cliché goes, is a healer. The bears buried themselves in snow and I buried myself in work and parenting. In so doing, it dawned on me that my grudge was illogical. In addition to hanging delectable birdseed within easy reach, I had hung a suet cake. It takes a firm act of will for me not to take a bite out of suet when I'm hanging it, especially the ones labeled "berry delicious" or "peanut delight." So I can only imagine how they must tempt bears, with smelling powers roughly two thousand times better than my own. Relegated to bland beetles and the occasional carcass all summer, a mere sniff of suet must send torrents of saliva down their jowls; especially bruins with hibernation on the mind. If I pass by an unguarded reception table on my college campus, I snatch donuts, cookies, cheese, whatever's offered. And if nobody's within sight, I even jam a few extras in my bag for later. We all know a pitiful guy like that. I happen to be him. My actions are instinctual and impulsive, undeterred by morality. If I'm driven by greed and gluttony, how can I blame bears for acting similarly?

This past May, I awoke from my philosophical hibernation. I was resolved to replace my feeder and end my blatant hypocrisy. Tractor Supply Co. devoted an entire spacious aisle to variously styled birdfeeders. Puny ones for $6.99, all the way up to colossal contraptions capable of feeding half the birds in my county. Fancying myself an average Joe, I opted for a $21.99 middle-of-the-road design. The particular one I chose was slightly garish, gabled, and hexagonal. It boasted a gazebo motif that seemed to say, "Yeah, I've arrived." I was upgrading;

this was way better than the homemade feeders of my youth, the waste bins I utilized in college, and the garage sale feeders of my graduate days. Sure, there were cheaper and sturdier feeders. But life is short. I wanted style. This one—with all its plastic and Plexiglas—had panache. I knew my practical minivan years were closing in. With this purchase, I would hold them at bay for one more season.

To justify my expense and rationalize my misgivings, I promised myself this would be my last feeder. Starting now and forevermore, I'd be a bona fide feeder steward. No bear will get its paws on this baby, I thought smugly the next day as I ran a steel cable from my roof to the trunk of a large red pine. With the cable in place, I climbed to the top of a stepladder and affixed the feeder about midway along it. I got out my ruler and measured. Nine feet and a few inches. Yes, we'd have to crane our necks a bit for the birds. But at least I'd have peace of mind. A bipedal polar bear could grab it, I reasoned. Or maybe a black bear waving a cane. If either of those things happened, I'd have bigger problems on my hands than broken birdfeeders.

Proud of my aerial engineering and always eager for accolades, I called to Ezra, who had appeared on the lawn in the midst of my tinkering. "Ez," I said, folding up the stepladder. "This feeder is yours. I'm giving it to you." It was a facade. This gesture was more sinister than benevolent. With feeder ownership, I hoped Ezra would become more invested in our joint birding enterprise. Perhaps, I calculated, I could eventually turn over the weekly refilling task to him.

"Thanks Dad!" Ez replied as he scampered away with his plastic bow and arrow, a toy insidiously designed to torture siblings. For the next month, Ezra seemed as happy about the new snazzy feeder as did the birds. They flitted about madly, posing like runway models during our family dinners. This feeder needed a "no vacancy" sign. Many others, lower down in the pecking order, were forced to wait impatiently on the steel cable, biding their time. With such a birdy bonanza, I didn't even bother with suet.

But a month of bounty was all I got. Much like the previous fall, I awoke one morning in June to a scene of utter carnage. My feeder, my garish, gabled, hexagonal feeder with a gazebo motif, lay scattered on the ground like a roadkill picked apart by scavengers. Distraught, I ran out to it. The Plexiglas was punctured in four places spaced equally apart. Like the last time, plastic shards adorned the lawn like party confetti. Other shards formed a Hansel and Gretel trail through the yard, the last piece lying near the woods. Everything else was untouched and serene. My feeder, my chintzy contraption that told the world I'd arrived, had been violated. This time—having invested more—I had been violated too. Once again, I had become the victim of a hungry bear. And once again, my long-sequestered grudge—mixed with newfound rage—resurfaced.

I walked back to the feeder's broken body and stared up at the steel cable. It remained strong and suspended. I was bewildered. Unless bruins have mastered stepladders, stilts, or slingshots, there was only one way a bear could have pulled this off: a wildly inspired leap. It must have been spectacular under the harvest moon. Disgusted, I picked up my feeder like I would a carcass. Amazing. Critical pieces were gone. Yet it stubbornly hung together as if sutured with sinew. I stared at it. Could it—would it—possibly still hold seed?

I gathered a few of the largest plastic shards from the lawn and beelined for the garage. Laying the recalcitrant feeder on the workbench, I considered my options. Glue wouldn't do. Nor would wire. I scanned my dusty, cobwebbed shelves, my eyes coming to rest on the one resource I'd been prone to hoard throughout my life: duct tape. Hmmm. An application of this standard silver duct tape would change everything. All aesthetics would be destroyed. But the feeder was pretty destroyed already. Duct tape was made for ducts. Not for keeping reading glasses together or holding front fenders on cars. And definitely not for holding bird feeders together. This was a clear either/or. Either patch the broken panels and sides with duct tape. Or scrap the feeder. So patch I did.

Job completed, I dumped in a gallon of seed. The sides sagged and the tape strained. Like the Union line at Gettysburg, it held. I strung the feeder back up and stepped back. From one side it looked fresh off the shelf. From the other, the hexagonal form had morphed into an irregular polygon. On cue, a chickadee alighted on the taped-up feeding deck. I smiled. If the birds didn't care about status symbols and aesthetics, neither would I. This time I would bear-proof the bejesus out of it. Nine feet increased to fifteen. Smugly, I folded up the stepladder and went back inside. The bears of western New York were smart. But as Jane Goodall would agree, primates were smarter than ursids.

That night at dinner, I realized a loophole in my logic. The problem wasn't that the birds didn't like the treetop feeder; they liked it a lot. The problem was that now it was so high we could no longer see them. Pride prevented me from pointing this out. Sitting there slurping up soup, I silently resolved to fix it. The simple solution hit me in the wee hours of the night. I chided myself for not thinking of it sooner. The steel cable needed to be *adjustable*.

The next morning—Saturday—I set to work. Perched again atop my ladder, I looped the steel cable around a stout branch on the same red pine and then worked it down the trunk.

Shoot. The cable was about five feet too short. I ran to the garage and rummaged. There, coiled on a nail, was the answer: a piece of wire from some sort of defunct electronics that likely dated to the 1950s. Repurposed wire seemed a nice complement to my never-say-die feeder. I affixed the cable to the wire and hammered three large nails into the tree. From the ground, in one easy motion, I could raise or lower the feeder to three different levels. Level one was for filling. Level two was for daytime birding. And each evening, I'd raise the feeder to bear-proof level three, fifteen feet high. The only bear that would reach it would be one launched from a cannon.

At that moment, Linda stepped outside to sweep the deck. Perfect timing.

"Hey, Linda! Watch this!" She paused, looking over. Smiling widely, I lowered the feeder to level one, then raised it to level two, and then . . . SNAP!

Blasted gravity! The feeder, freshly full of seed, fell like a bowling ball. THUD. Upon hitting the ground, the feeder's gazebo roof blasted off and birdseed shot out the top like low-budget fireworks. My repurposed wire from the 1950s had lost its purpose.

One of my annoying habits is to search for meaning in all things, both large and small. Instantly the haplessly mangled body of my feeder became an overt metaphor for my life: well-intentioned, yes. Otherwise impractical, defunct, and utterly ineffectual.

"This is my life!" I shouted to Linda. She stood motionless on the deck, unsure how to respond. Undeserving of empathy, I slunk back to the garage, marched straight to my large trashcan, whipped off the lid, and dangled the ill-conceived, ill-advised, and ill-fated feeder over the top.

I couldn't let go. I simply stood there in suspended animation.

I search for meaning and metaphor. I also search for symbolism, melodramatic or otherwise. This moment was just that. Letting go cemented my incompetence. Clinging like the last leaf on an autumn maple symbolized something else. To rational folks, holding onto this feeder symbolized compounding stupidity and grievous recalcitrance. To me, fully ensnared in the absurdity of the moment, it symbolized hope, tenacity, and a chance for redemption.

My jaw relaxed. Color returned to my cheeks. I went back to my workbench and spread the wreckage out. Without the slightest hesitation, I grabbed the duct tape and started the delicate process of mummification. With every wrap, I said goodbye to my garish, gabled, hexagonal feeder with a gazebo motif. The feeder I'd longed for—the one that subtly told the world that I'd arrived—was no more. In its place lay a silver mummy, one with noticeable scoliosis. A visual travesty—a Frankenstein of feeders.

What happened next was graciously profound. Despite her deep love of aesthetics and Cartesian order, Linda suggested I rehang the feeder at the original scene of the bear and broken cable crimes. Even though this backyard blight stood in full view of our dinner table.

The mummified feeder still hangs today. And Linda continues to accept it. Perhaps she wills herself not to look out the window anymore. Or perhaps she's glad I'm not blowing any more money on feeders. I don't ask her. Because I like to think her acceptance stands for something grander. There, tenuously suspended from a steel cable, sways our very own medley of metaphor and symbolism enmeshed in reality. A metaphor for hapless determination. A symbol of our optimistic resourcefulness. And the reality of sharing our space with equally determined and resourceful creatures. Creatures leading precarious lives that mirror our own. They also need food and shelter and space. They ask for little. The least I can give them is a fair shake.

I am determined to grant them this. They've given me so much: joy, wonder, knowledge, and most recently—humility. Humility harvested from seeds of frustration and cultivated through coexistence; a simple recognition of the rights of other species. So just as I've hung up my feeder, I've hung up my grudge. With a handy roll of duct tape, I'll strive to accommodate all the creatures that flit and lumber through my yard. I'll try to be smarter, yes. But the next time I'm outwitted, I won't have another existential crisis. I'll just grin and bear it.

26 · CLUTCH PERFORMANCE

I feel most deeply that the whole subject is too profound for the human intellect. A dog might as well speculate on the mind of Newton.

—Charles Darwin

I've been thinking about clutch size lately. This probably happens to lots of couples in their mid-thirties. Linda and I had two kids already—a boy and a girl—so things seemed pretty settled. But every now and then, the question fluttered by like a fritillary. What about a third? After all, three did seem more complete than two. When questions like this arise, I tend to ask around and seek consensus.

"You'll be outnumbered—you shouldn't!"

"They'll keep each other company—you should!"

"You'll never travel again—you shouldn't!"

"A family of five is perfect—you should!"

Consensus was not to be found; all my friends had different opinions. When people fail me—for good or ill—I tend to turn back to the birds. So here I am again.

While I've always enjoyed finding bird nests, my interest has been heightened of late. I'm no longer content to make a note of the nest and leave. Now whenever I find a nest, I count eggs or fledglings or both. Obsessively. Since I too am brooding, the number of young ones has become all-important.

So it was of little surprise last spring, while getting out of my truck at the entrance of Rattlesnake Hill Wildlife Management Area in New York, that I noticed an active blue-headed vireo nest. It was tightly woven into a fork in a spindly maple about twenty feet off the ground. Having filled a notebook with years of robin statistics (two to three broods of four eggs each in my corner of western New York, if you're curious), I simply had to see how many kids a vireo desires.

I eyed the tree. Its diameter rivaled a table leg. Doable? Maybe. Only one way to find out. With one last hike of my pants I shimmied up. The higher I got, the more the tree bent. The vireo remained stoical and nonplussed. One thing was clear; this wouldn't work. I slid back down and stared up at the nest. The vireo stared back impassively. For reasons I can't explain to non-biologists, I really wanted this data. *Needed* it. My day, my notebook, my life suddenly seemed incomplete without it. But how could I get it? As I often do when I have a quandary, I sat down on my truck's hood, took out my travel mug of tepid coffee, and hatched a plan.

The first thing I needed was for the vireo to leave. Ten long minutes later, it finally flew off. Not knowing when it would return, I sprang into action. Hastily, I drove my truck under the nest, parked it, and climbed atop the roof. Even on tip-toes, I couldn't get my chin above the nest. Fortunately, gangly arms accompany my six-foot-two frame. Reaching my arm up high, my camera just made it over the lip of the nest. Blindly, I snapped a few photos. Checking my screen, I counted three pearly white eggs and one oversized, splotchy-brown egg.

A textbook case of brood parasitism. This phenomenon occurs when a bird lays one or more eggs into the nest of another bird and expects that bird to incubate the eggs and raise the chicks free of charge. If the egg dumper dupes the host, it's untethered from a season of feathered bondage. It can repeat its duplicity, or fritter away its spring days watching soaps. It's another story for the duped. Not only do they waste their days raising another's chick, they often lose their own in the process. Babies of brood parasites tend to hatch faster, grow quicker, and as a result, dominate the host's own chicks. Foster parents can't seem to resist the color of the gape flanges, the ruby-red mouth linings, and the other food-soliciting beacons the parasite chicks employ.

Nature may be red in tooth and claw. For newborn brood parasites, it's red in back and feet. Parasitic cowbird chicks, for example, hatch first and instinctively throw it in reverse using their oversized feet. Nest cameras have revealed bloodcurdling footage of freshly hatched, naked pink cowbird babies methodically ejecting the host's eggs out of the nest with the help of their concavely shaped backs. Cowbird babies don't waste precious time crying. They get right down to the first order of the day, homicide.

It's either clever or conniving, depending on which bird you relate to. I tend to think it's both, especially when I consider the in-depth, devilish ways some brood parasites have for slipping eggs into others' nests. Who needs Ocean's eleven when two will suffice? Some female parasites hide in the vegetation while the mate flies up to the host nest, intentionally drawing attention. The hosts recognize the intruders and invariably give chase. Such subterfuge allows the furtive female parasite to slide in, lay an egg, and depart before the host returns. More often than not, she grabs one of the host's eggs as she leaves, ensuring the number remains the same. It's less suspicious that way.

The splotchy-brown egg in the vireo nest was most certainly laid by a cowbird. Brown-headed cowbirds are America's most common brood parasite, laying eggs in the nests of more than 220 species. Their duplicitous ways have long given them a bad rep. But there is nothing villainous about parasitism; it's just another viable strategy for raising young, devious though it may seem. Cowbirds shouldn't be blamed; natural selection should, as it's the force that has produced it. But that's ridiculous. The real guilty party—cough, cough—is us. Cowbirds were historically limited to the short-grass plains of the United States and Canada. One of the greatest skills of *Homo sapiens*, however, is the ability to fragment and convert large expanses of land. We've done this with aplomb, homogenizing the environment into sprawling agricultural and suburban landscapes. In so doing, we've opened the forests and passed out party invitations to all willing cowbirds. They've readily accepted, expanding far into the east and exposing naïve populations and new bird species to parasitism.

The blue-headed vireo was just such a victim of the cowbirds' range expansion. If this particular cowbird chick failed to kill his stepbrothers and stepsisters, the vireo parents would raise at least four young this summer, including the forced adoption. I made a mental note, jumped off the roof of my truck, and let the vireo nest be. She flew back moments later none the wiser, making me think that I, too, would make a good parasite (Linda would gleefully affirm this hunch). I jotted down the data and drove off. In a few short days, Mr. and Mrs. Vireo would have their hands—or wings—full indeed.

Just a few weeks before my encounter with the vireos, I was traipsing along a rocky island trail forty kilometers off the Ecuadorian mainland. The island was perfect for eager, financially challenged groups like my ornithology class. Known as Poor Man's Galapagos, the island was less expensive to visit but still offered plenty to see. Before we'd arrived in Ecuador, I had lectured at length about the majesty and well, length, of the albatross. The wingspan of the wandering albatross is the longest in the world, measuring eleven feet eleven inches. Nearly two feet longer than a basketball hoop! To drive the point home, I'd brought a tape measure to class and had two students extend it to the albatross's wingspan. It stretched well beyond the horizontal chalkboard, nearly wall to wall. Everybody gasped.

Having logged a week in the jungle upon arrival, my students were now dreaming of albatrosses. With the strained budget that we had, Poor Man's Galapagos was our only remaining hope. My students and I shared an oversized imagination. Upon stepping off the boat, we'd expected dozens of these pterodactyl-sized birds to be swooping around our heads. Fat chance. After a nauseating boat ride and a three-hour hike, we'd found frigate birds, boobies, and tropicbirds, but neither bill nor bum of an albatross.

Needing to return to the mainland, we headed toward our boat. Just then a weathered old man came ambling down our dirt path. He held a finger to his lips. "There's a waved albatross just ahead," he whispered, nodding slightly.

Ecstatic, we surged ahead, watching the skies. We should have been staring down. I skidded to a halt. At my feet was a massive, pearly white bird. Not expecting a sudden stop and still looking up, my students rammed into me. Nobody apologized. We had found the species we'd sought! A waved albatross. Not quite the monster the wandering albatross is, but a giant seabird nonetheless. We formed a semi-circle around the bird, expecting it to stand up and do something grand and albatross-ish. Seconds ticked by. Then minutes. The albatross remained curled up on the dusty trail fast asleep. Its head was tucked tidily into its coverts and the only eye we could see seemed utterly apathetic to our presence. Sitting on the ground like a jumbo-sized watermelon, the sedate bird was nothing like the one that had flown through our minds. Impressive, yes. But action-wise, this bird was decidedly subpar. The island's long-tailed mockingbird had been far more inspiring. During the entire ten minutes we watched, the albatross moved only once. For me, the movement was critical because it allowed a brief look at one gleaming white egg wedged underneath.

An egg! In several weeks or maybe a month, that egg would break open and a ravenous chick would emerge; one that would demand constant food and fellowship. Unlike the vireos I later found in New York, this albatross would raise just one. If food was abundant, this lone, little chick might be spoiled rotten.

Realizing this encounter had all the excitement of watching paint dry, we granted the albatross a wide berth and continued on down the trail. My mind wandered. The wild turkey nest I'd stumbled upon while picking blackberries two summers previous popped up. "Nest" didn't describe the scene I'd found there in western New York; it was more of an egg depot—eleven white, golf-ball-sized eggs scattered on the ground. And unlike our experience with the albatross, my approach had caused the mother turkey to shoot off through the forest like a feathered cannonball. Rural New York was no island. And I was just another likely predator. One that surely wouldn't turn down a platter of scrambled eggs.

* * *

Now removed from these experiences, I'm left with my notebooks of random data, the portly reference books making my shelves sag, and a lot of questions. Here's what I know: One, there are about ten thousand species of birds. Two, they're abundant. Some, like the red-billed quelea of Africa, number in the billions. And three, they've been good at what they do for a really long time. Since birds are dinosaurs, they've been around about a hundred million years or so. Obviously, birds come through in the clutch.

What is a clutch, for that matter? Basically, a clutch is the number of eggs laid in a single breeding attempt. Despite this simple definition, determining clutch size is no simple affair.

It's influenced by a host of complicating variables such as predation rates, geography, egg-laying dates, and the female's condition, among many others.

Take predation, for example. Islands tend to have fewer predators. So birds like albatrosses can afford to lay fewer eggs because their eggs have a higher chance for survival. On Poor Man's Galapagos, we stood only a few feet away from our incubating albatross without it even lifting an eyelid. Apathy confirmed. Meanwhile, at the turkey nest, I struck abject terror into the poor hen's palpitating heart. Rightfully so. Turkey-egg-snatching predators are legion: from foxes, coyotes, and bobcats, to weasels, raccoons, and crows.

The turkey's decision to lay eleven eggs isn't simple either. Fortunately, evolution has made it for her. Large clutch sizes can spread out risk. If a few eggs get eaten, broken, or diseased, maybe the others will survive. Large clutches can intensify risk too, by conspicuously attracting predators. Had the turkey laid one egg in the leaf litter instead of eleven, I doubt I would have noticed the nest. Even the vireo, with a less visible nest than the turkey, had fallen victim to an egg-snatcher, a cowbird that had likely replaced a vireo egg with one of its own.

Another basic variable like geography is similarly complex. Clutch sizes tend to be smaller the closer one gets to the equator. Why? Because food supply tends to be more consistent throughout the year in the tropics. Based on this, you might think females would lay larger clutches because they can accurately predict how much food they'll find in the fridge for their young. Not so fast. Since food is more consistent near the equator, bird populations also tend to reach optimum densities. So these steady, year-round resources have to be divvied up more. With a higher density of birds all sharing a resource, there is naturally less food available for each species' chicks. The result? Smaller clutches across the board.

And then, of course, there's the possibility of brood parasitism, which is alarmingly common in the tropics. All this to say, when birds are thinking about family planning, they have a lot to consider, too. Just think, all this handwringing—wing-wringing, rather—happens before an egg even hatches. Determining clutch size is the easy part! Once the clutch hatches, a brood—a family of young birds—begins. That's the hard part.

So how does all this help Linda and me as we contemplate a larger brood? Well, the turkey model is definitely out. Eleven babies would make us more distraught than the panicked hen I kicked up. The albatross model is out, too. It isn't bad; it's just that we've already eclipsed its paltry one-chick clutch. That leaves us with the vireo. The nest I inspected revealed three biological offspring and one adoptee. Sounds ideal. But, could we pay the weekly grocery bill? Could we grant them all adequate opportunities? Would we need to put an addition on the house? Would they get along? Could we maintain our sanity? Would they ever leave the nest?

Hold on. Too many questions. Too many variables and hypotheticals. I've brooded long enough. Perhaps I'll forego peeking into any more bird nests and amassing more data. And give the footstool-sized books a break too. I'm ready for cruise control, to go automatic. If the birds have taught me anything, it's to lay off the clutch.

27 · FRUSTRATION OR FERVOR

The real voyage of discovery consists not of seeking new landscapes, but in having new eyes.

—Marcel Proust

We all have a friend like this. A friend who has more time, more money, and more opportunities. This friend also happens to like birds. And likes to tell you about them. It seems like every other month, you get another email chronicling the latest adventure. Every email mentions mystical-sounding birds like resplendent quetzal and vulturine guineafowl. Every email also has a number buried somewhere within: 88, 196, 304. Even without explanation, you know exactly what these numbers refer to: new birds seen. With every note, your friend's life list grows. Yours remains virtually unchanged from last year. And the year before that. You did manage to finally find a vesper sparrow after a two-hour drive last May. And your dog flushed a Wilson's snipe this spring. But that's it. Two new birds. Whoopee.

After several weeks of letting it lie dormant in your inbox, you force yourself to hit reply. Congratulations, you write. You fill a paragraph with hollow lines, mention your sparrow and snipe, and talk about the cute family of robins nesting on your windowsill. While the body of your letter is short on enthusiasm, your ending is sincere: sure wish I could join you one of these years, you write, adding an exclamation mark.

But you can't. You are besieged by the typical triumvirate of travails: time, money, and responsibilities. Your job is like a python swallowing whatever time you have. Spare money? Nope. That's allotted for a new roof for the garage. Besides, your kids are in soccer leagues all summer. And you can't forget about the ever-growing mold problem in the basement. Or the braces your daughter needs. Your dream of a swollen life list marked with blue-crowned mot-mots and fiery minivets will have to wait for retirement. If your Social Security comes through, that is.

Face it. You're trapped in your county with little more than the usual suspects—robins, sparrows, and starlings.

You have two options: frustration, or fervor. The path of frustration is a tired one. It operates from the mindset of "I've already seen it all" and, "There's nothing left to learn here." If you choose this path, your binoculars feel heavy, if you bother bringing them. Your field notes go unmarked for weeks, or even years. Oh look, another oriole, you think to yourself, barely breaking stride along your walk that rarely deviates from the day before.

The path of fervor, however, operates from a wholly different mindset, one of intellectual infancy. Yes, you've seen and learned a lot. But whoa, why is that oriole so splotchy? Is it a juvenile? If so, when did it fledge? Why is it gleaning insects from that shrub like a warbler? I thought they sipped nectar and ate jelly! Why did that yellow warbler just enter that bush? There must be a nest. Yes, here it is! Oh my, almost the entire cuplike structure is made of deer hair. Do they always use deer hair? Shouldn't there be eggs by now? Last year's notes say there should. Perhaps this extended cold snap is responsible. Or did a chipmunk get them?

The difference between frustration and fervor is palpable. I've ventured down both paths. My frustration peaked with the birth of my second child. Suddenly, literally overnight, all my birding freedom flew south. When I wasn't at work, I was with the kids. And when I was with the kids, I certainly wasn't seeing new birds. Even if the rare opportunity to bird did arrive, I lacked the energy to go.

Hope for me arrived in the form of a random anecdote about an old painting and a few pithy insights from a few keen-eyed naturalists. Together, this odd concoction has rerouted my dreary course. First the anecdote.

In 1861, Frederic Edwin Church unveiled a massive painting called *The Icebergs*, in New York. The reaction to the six-by-ten-foot-wide arctic landscape scene was as quiet as the painting itself. Nor did it fare much better when the painting was exhibited in Boston. It finally generated acclaim overseas, when it arrived in London.

Just as soon as the painting was appreciated, something weird happened. After being purchased, it disappeared for 116 years. Somehow, *The Icebergs* went missing as it passed by inheritance through several generations. It reappeared mysteriously, hanging frameless in a stairwell of a reform school for boys in England. During one of the decades it hung there, one of the boys took the liberty of signing it. Short of funds, the school sent the work to the United States where it was auctioned in 1979. Church's work sold for a record $2.5 million in the very country that hadn't appreciated it. Now it proudly hangs in the Dallas Museum of Fine Arts.

The message here is simple. With fresh eyes, the mundane becomes marvelous. Here on my three acres in the rural western New York countryside, all the beauty of a masterful painting surrounds me. For too long I was a boy in the reform school, cruising past it day after day and never appreciating its unparalleled worth. At long last, my time came to reform.

With the constant lure of the exotic and far-off, how did I start to appreciate what I have? It started with implementing—

not just understanding—John Burroughs's idea when he wrote the simple sentence: "There is news in every bush." Emulating Burroughs is realizing that nature appreciation is in the eye of the beholder. Three acres, which seemed so measly before, burst forth this year with sixty-four birds, each with wildly unique life histories! Turns out I'm living in the Fertile Crescent. Fledglings are swarming the place. The house wrens alone have brought out a dozen wide-eyed whippersnappers. Now on the path to fervor, news isn't just in every bush, it's in every building. This spring alone, I've had a starling nest in the siding, a skunk under the shed, a Carolina wren in the garage, and raccoons in the car (they really like Wheat Thins, it turns out). We are cohabitating with creatures. Along my new path, such nuisances have metamorphized into curiosities.

It's true that motmots and minivets still flutter through my dreams. But I don't wake up frustrated anymore. There's no time for that when there's so much to learn. I mean, doesn't that rose-breasted grosbeak call I'm hearing out the window sound odd? Is this a new dialect? Or is it a juvenile trying out its syrinx for the first time? Do the males and females both sing?

The next time I check email, I'll likely have another email from my ever-traveling, ever-listing friend whose life I will never have. Instead of feeling jealous, I'll remember Samuel Johnson's words: "traveling widely in one's neighborhood is the greatest of journeys." For what I may lack in birding breadth, I can make up for in depth. Right here at home.

"The land knows you," wrote Robin Wall Kimmerer, "even when you are lost." Now I'm finally reciprocating with my home plot, deepening my land relationship. The result? Far less frustration and a lot more joy. Joy that comes with uncovering new parts of creation and my relationship to it. Another great naturalist, Henry David Thoreau, once famously penned that he traveled widely in Concord. Although I'm sure Thoreau was being tongue-in-cheek, I aim to copy him nonetheless. Except that I'm traveling widely in my own yard. And I need to get going. Because three acres is much more than just a lot.

28 · JUST BECAUSE

*"To be thousands of miles from home and friends, hot,
tired, dirty, breathless with pursuit, but holding in my
hand and gloating over some new and rare bird, I feel
a sort of charitable pity for the rest of the world."*

—Elliott Coues

Some people love chocolate. Others love puppies. Me? I love range maps in field guides. I like them so much that when I open a bird book, I often notice the miniscule and marginal range map before I notice the big, colorful painting of the bird to which the map belongs. I'm not sure why. Perhaps because the maps are besmeared in various eye-catching hues. Or maybe it's their sheer particularity. Some span whole continents, while others take on weird amoeba-like shapes with gaps and sometimes even question marks in the middle.

If pressed, however, the maps I love best are the ones that show really, really tiny ranges. Like the map that depicts the range of Kirtland's warbler. This dapper little bird nests only in regenerating jack pine groves in northern Michigan. So if the map in question depicts the continental United States, this bird gets the smallest of dots, a mere period on an otherwise empty page. With a bird like Kirtland's, you have to bring the book closer to your face or stare over the top of your glasses. On computer screens, the zoom function is indispensable. Small as they are, tiny species locales on range maps often catch my attention faster than a stop sign on a little-traveled country road. And they're far more likely to stop me in my tracks.

In my half-baked way of seeing the world, these little dots represent the dreamiest of destinations. They are the fine print in my Lonely Planet guide, often signifying a place far off the beaten path with few people and unique habitat. As I'm sure Robert Frost would agree, these little dots lie at end of the road less traveled by.

But traveling with twenty-five college students in Tanzania requires regular meals, some semblance of lodging, and frequent bathroom breaks. As the leader, I need to know where I'm going. I can't afford to take the road less traveled by. Or any road less traveled by, for that matter. As in many developing countries, lightly traveled roads are lightly traveled for a reason; they are pot-holed, miry, and in the rainy season at least, often impassable. Chalking it up as uncharacteristic wisdom, I had long ignored these roads in Tanzania. All except one, that is. At the end of one particular road, according to a range map in my trusty *Field Guide to the Birds of East Africa*, was a little innocuous dot.

In this particular field guide, the dot was indeed blood red. As such, it burned like a hot ember in my book. As much as I distracted myself with daily life, I couldn't seem to snuff it out. Any casual thumbing through this bird book would eventually leave me stuck in the weaver section, staring at the dainty dot. It belonged to the Kilombero weaver of Tanzania. As far as weavers go, this one is decidedly average. Like its dozens of brethren in East Africa, the Kilombero weaver is yellow and weaves a nifty nest it suspends from tall rank grass growing in or along watercourses. Like a bank robber, the male conceals his identity with a small black mask.

The Kilombero weaver is decidedly not average in one key respect. Unlike most weavers, this one is a serious recluse.

It is such a homebody, in fact, that it lives out its days in one particular marsh in the south-central part of the country. Nor does the bird ever migrate. Unsurprisingly, this weaver evaded detection by western eyes for centuries. So once it was finally found—in 1991—it was called the "Kilombero" weaver for its highly specific and difficult-to-reach locale. Kirtland's warbler is a downright cosmopolitan compared to the Kilombero clan.

The little red dot sucked me in with the force of a black hole. Unable to resist any longer, I seized upon a rare gap in my schedule, left the students behind, and rattled down the road less traveled by. After three hours of lurching and leaning, my land cruiser reached the mighty Kilombero River. Crossing the river requires driving onto an antiquated ferry. Today there was no ferry to be found. Woefully overloaded, the ferry had flipped that very morning and was resting at the bottom of the river like an aquarium decoration. Many vehicles had sunk with it. One of them, I discovered, was an armored bank car. Seizing a rare opportunity to get rich quickly, dozens of fishermen had plunged into the flooded river to retrieve whatever booty they could. Resourceful, yes. Also highly questionable. In response, the Tanzanian army had been deployed and was now barring access to a large section of the river. Including the part we had planned on visiting.

I immediately assumed my quest had ended with this unusual bit of bad luck. Not so, smiled my optimistic guide, Emmanuel. We hadn't driven all this way to shrug our shoulders and give up. Yes, the Kilombero weaver was restricted to this small spot, but maybe the bird had another colony or two further upriver. Traveling any further by land, however, was out of the question. El Nino had made sure of that. All we needed to do, Emmanuel explained, was hop in a dugout and paddle upriver. No big deal.

For a risk-averse person like me, this was definitely a big

deal. I quickly considered the four unexpected variables: A sunken ferry. A Tanzanian army blockade, El Nino flooding. A dugout. None of these were good omens. Then I looked at Emmanuel's irrepressible grin.

"Who can take us?" I asked, surprising even myself. I held out hope. Surely nobody would dare paddle in this current.

"I know a guy . . ." Emmanuel said, too excited to finish his sentence. With that he spun on his heels and disappeared into a throng of curious onlookers.

Emmanuel did in fact know a guy. Because ten minutes later I was wedged into a leaky dugout canoe. It appeared to have been made out of a sapling, the top so narrow it prevented my pelvis from entering. To make it work, I'd have to sit high up, like riding atop a camel when you're used to horses. Our skipper, a grizzled Tanzanian man who looked as old and cracked as the boat, wordlessly handed me a faded plastic crate. I flipped it over and tried to get comfortable, balancing my camera, binoculars, and several thousand dollars of cash—which I couldn't afford to leave unattended in the car—on top of my shoes. Why on top of my shoes? To keep my stuff from floating away . . . in the boat.

Before we'd even pushed off from shore, putrid black water soaked through the sides of my porous shoes. A dozen paddle strokes later we entered the main current, the point of no return. I had trusted everything—equipment, money, my very life—on the skills of this ancient mariner. I sought his face for reassurance. What I found was just that—absolute tranquility. He looked straight ahead, revealing neither worry nor fear, an unlit cigarette miraculously clinging to his lower lip as if affixed with superglue. His massive calloused hands, which dwarfed the handle of his crude wooden paddle, resembled rhino hide. Catching my anxious eyes he flashed me a wide, one-toothed smile. How one tooth had survived while all the others had not was a mystery. One thing was clear though. This man was utterly at home here in this undersized dugout on this oversized river. Like the weaver I was risking all to see, this old man was a rare endemic.

I've brushed shoulders with enough people to realize that I'm by no means the only nutjob on Earth. We dubious decision-makers are sprinkled throughout. This comforts me and I take solace knowing that had I been born one or two hundred years earlier, I'd be judged perfectly sane. Wedging myself in a diminutive dugout was nothing!

Far more insane, for example, was Charles Bendire. In 1872, thirty-five-year-old Charles was horseback riding through southern Arizona as a member of the US Cavalry when he spied a zone-tailed hawk, a rare species with a limited range. With a few tugs on the reins, Charles was soon galloping down his own road less traveled by, if there was a road at all. The hawk soon alighted near its nest in a large cottonwood. Charles climbed up the tree, grabbed the only egg he saw, and vowed to return again once the hawk had laid another.

A week or so later, Charles made good his vow. In the midst of grabbing two more eggs, he glanced down and shuddered. Several Apache Indians were hidden not far away, watching him from the confines of a small canyon. Cool-headed Charles climbed down, casually cradling the eggs as he did so, so as not to alert the Indians that he'd spied them. Perhaps, he reasoned, this would stave off their attack. As soon as he touched the ground, he ended his casual pretense. Instantly, he jumped on his horse and took off at a breakneck pace for camp. The Apache men gave chase.

Charles had two goals. One was to preserve his life. The second was to preserve the eggs for his friend Spencer Fullerton Baird, then with the Smithsonian Museum. Charles may have lost his marbles. But he didn't lose his eggs. Rather, he popped them in his mouth like gobstoppers. For five miles he galloped, his cheeks bulging as he painstakingly tried to breathe without busting the eggs. Not only did he evade his pursuers and preserve the eggs, but he also managed to partially incubate one in his mouth. His only setback was sore jaw muscles; pain lingered for several days thereafter. Bendire's thrasher, a rare bird of the Southwest, seems an especially apt eponym for this wild-eyed birdman.

Equally insane, and far less likeable by most accounts, was Elliott Coues. Like Bendire, Coues loved nature and was collecting for the Smithsonian. He also spent a lot of time trying to sidestep the Apache people in the American Southwest. One day, Coues chanced upon a rare subspecies of rattlesnake. Desiring the skin for the museum, Coues dispatched it. A band of Apache warriors justifiably upset over past treatment by the US Army, surprised Coues while in the act of filleting the snake. They gave chase, intent on capturing him.

Quick-thinking Coues had only moments to react. Brazenly (stupidly?) he finished stripping off the snakeskin. Unlike Bendire's eggs, this wouldn't fit in his mouth. Instead, he wrapped the still-bleeding skin around his gun barrel. With the skin in place, he made off like a bandit, barely outrunning the Apache fighters behind him.

Coues might have contributed far more to science if his friends had valued sobriety. Short on preservatives, Coues was forced to store many rare wildlife specimens in rum. One infamous night when Coues was away, his comrades drank his precious keg dry, ruining his many specimens in the process. I can't help but wonder: is this where the expression "having a frog in the throat" comes from?

The bizarre accounts of Bendire and Coues lend me comfort. It is nice knowing that other men make dumb decisions for questionable returns. But there was one big difference between their accounts and mine. While theirs were split-second decisions, I'd had time. And now I was stuck in a protracted moment of anxiety. I was literally stuck, wedged into my dugout without any means of escape. We crept upriver at a snail's pace, hugging the shore to avoid the strongest current. We moved rhythmically, like a hesitant chameleon, as the sun beat down on my tense body. The old man paddled and paddled, the heat and the motion hypnotizing us all. Banter ebbed and then diminished altogether. Gradually, I retreated deeper and deeper into myself. Sometime during this dreamlike trance, the full force of the question hit. *Why?*

Why was I in Africa? Why was I in a slowly sinking dugout? Why was I chasing a bird? Why, for heaven's sake, did I care about seeing a Kilombero weaver?

The rhetorical questions blanketed me like a heavy, opaque veil. I attempted to answer them nonetheless. Why was I in Africa? Well, it was part of my job. Good. One down. Why was I in a slowly sinking dugout? That one was harder. Why was I chasing a bird? Hmmm . . . why did I want to see a Kilombero weaver? Because . . . because . . . oh, forget it. Answers were as hard to come by as shade. It felt like reaching into a pocket and only finding lint.

Such moments are not unfamiliar to parents with overly inquisitive children. Why is the sky blue? Well, because molecules in the air scatter blue light from the sun more than they scatter the other colors. Why do molecules scatter blue light? Well that's because blue light waves are shorter than the waves of the other colors. But why are blue light waves shorter? Because . . . because . . . I don't know, okay! Just because!

It's never satisfactory. But it's true. There's a limit to the explanations we can give. Things are because they are. And without Aristotle or Kant or God on speed dial, we're all stuck in leaky dugouts of our own. "What is it that brings me here to stand like a rock in this river of sound?" ethnobotanist Robin Wall Kimmerer asked in *Gathering Moss*. I can't help but wonder what prompted her question. Or if she was able to answer it. Sleuthing out ultimate reasons for the color of the sky or what brought you to stand in a river is difficult, perhaps even futile.

Since ultimate reasons are often as murky as the river, we're left with a mixed bag of the proximate. Why was I in a leaky dugout with now thoroughly soaked shoes? The proximate explanation is that I wanted to be. I was chasing a bird because I cared about birds. And I cared about the Kilombero weaver because, well, Kilombero weavers were undeniably cool. Their range maps, the itsy bitsy bulls-eye, added to their mystique.

I knew Kilombero weavers were cool. Now I know why. Because at that very moment, lost in my metaphysical maze, a flesh and blood Kilombero weaver flew across the bow of the boat. A long blade of grass dangled in its bill like a linguine noodle. The lemon-yellow bird landed in some overhanging vegetation along the river's edge and set to work weaving it into an intricate onion-shaped nest. The weaver flapped vigorously, hanging upside down as his nest bobbed a few feet above the river's surface. The focused bird finished threading the blade like a well-practiced tailor and then disappeared into the reeds. Put a gun to my head and I doubt I could replicate the weaver's feat. Opposable thumbs notwithstanding.

The weaver had flown over my boat with a blade of grass. It seemed more like a dove returning with an olive branch. It symbolized that my ark of vexing questions—and hopefully this dugout—would soon come to rest.

My dumb decisions are inexcusable. They're inexplicable, too. I think Bendire and Coues knew this over a century ago as I know it today. This didn't stop them from doing what they loved. Nor will it stop me. I got in a leaky dugout because I wanted to. I pursue nature because I care about it. And I care about it because, well, just because.

29. It's Not You, It's Me

I wanted movement and not a calm course of existence. I wanted excitement and danger and the chance to sacrifice myself for my love. I felt in myself a superabundance of energy which found no outlet in our quiet life.

—Leo Tolstoy

If a good first date is critical for a successful long-term relationship, then I never should have broken up with Yellowstone in the first place. It wasn't just good, it was wonderful; a one-night stand full of unfounded fear and zero regret. The rapturous details bear sharing.

The first step was picking a good place. The Soda Butte trailhead in the famous Lamar Valley proved a no-brainer. Flowers were blooming. Animals were bountiful. And the crisp June air was intoxicating. So at the immortal age of twenty-two, I left my small Toyota pickup at the trailhead, heaved on my monstrous pack, and headed in, ready to romance the wild.

The date did include a few awkward moments, however. The first being a broken elk antler I nearly tripped over. I had grown up in whitetail country. Deer antlers could be carried in one hand. Just one side of the elk's rack required two. I picked it up. Shoot, this could be used for arm curls. I replaced it on the ground and ran my fingers along its smooth, sun-bleached surface. If just one side of a rack is this big, then how big was the creature that carried it? More importantly, how big—or how vicious—was the animal that kills the creature that carries it? I resumed hiking, slightly alarmed by the increasing number of antlers, rib cages, and skulls lying about. My confidence remained, but I eyed the tree line.

That night I made my campfire exceptionally large. An inveterate introvert, I relished solitude. But not now. The valley walls, which seemed so welcoming in the day, had closed in oppressively. The fingernail moon offered little solace. Firelight flickered off the bleached carcasses littering the ground. "You'll love the campsite!" the ranger had exclaimed that morning. Why hadn't he also informed me it doubled as a mass grave? This wasn't a place that gave life; it was a place that snuffed it out.

My choice of this valley was strategic, predicated upon the bleak ecological record of the United States federal government. Having no apparent ecological value, wolves were systematically exterminated from much of the country, including parks. Yellowstone was no exception. The last wild wolves in the park—two unlucky pups discovered in the northeast corner—were killed in 1924. Without wolves, elk numbers exploded. A trophic cascade ensued, which is a fancy way of saying that wolf removal affected many species on down the food chain, often adversely. Thankfully, holistic thinkers like Aldo Leopold began speaking up, increasing environmental awareness. The tide slowly turned. After a long and heated debate lasting over a decade, fourteen wolves were captured in the Rocky Mountains of western Alberta and reintroduced into Yellowstone. The reintroduction worked. By 2001—my first date with the park—132 wild wolves roamed around the Greater Yellowstone Ecosystem. And where was this hotbed of wolf reintroduction and reestablishment? The Lamar Valley, of course.

Like lots of kids, I was captivated by wolves. Untold nights

I fell asleep in the cozy confines of my bedroom to *Algonquin Suite*, melodies punctuated by wolves. Over time, however, I'd grown weary of hearing wolf song from speakers. I craved the real thing, to drift off to a chorus of haunting howls.

How poorly I knew myself! Here, without anybody to manufacture bravado for, my childhood desire had vanished. The fire, which I continually fed, seemed my only friend. A grizzly was certainly pacing just beyond the firelight, patiently biding its time.

Sleepiness gradually overwhelmed my fear. I built up the fire as large as I could and reluctantly crawled into my tent. I yanked my knit hat as low as it would go and cinched up my sleeping bag so tight that only my nose showed. The four bedroom walls of my youth and my *Algonquin Suite* melodies seemed another world away. Who was I kidding? I wasn't ready for the real thing. Unable to see shadows or hear the night sounds, my imagination slowed and sleep mercifully enveloped me.

I smelled it before I saw it. The overwhelming odor of large animal. And then sounds, munching, deep and guttural. Only a colossal mouth could make these. Munch, munch, munch . . . Cinched in tightly in my sleeping bag, my arms remained pinned to my sides. Stealthy movement was impossible. So this is what a caterpillar feels like just before it's gobbled by a warbler. I lurched over, peering out the mesh screen of my tent. Three feet away, in the predawn gloaming, I caught a miniature image of myself. It was my reflection lodged in a large bulbous eyeball. As the pupil dilated, the munching ceased. Saliva-soaked grass slipped out of its mouth. The great head turned, shaggy strands of neck hair dragging in the dew. The glistening muzzle was bedecked with glittery droplets. Clouds of steam billowed out as it leveled one eye with my own. I dared neither breathe nor blink. I had fallen asleep in Yellowstone and awoken in Jurassic Park. This wasn't one of the predators that had stalked through my dreams. Park brochures had informed me that statistically, this one was far more lethal. A bison.

Less than a millimeter of mesh separated me from the whimsy of this 1,400-pound bulldozer. The facts were grim. A sneeze, a twitch, anything could provoke the beast. My prostrate form would be pulverized. Seconds ticked by. My elbows, supporting my weight, began aching from the stony ground. I clenched my teeth. Shifting positions was out of the question. Fortunately, the bison broke first.

HUMPF! Air blasted out its flaring nostrils. With startling swiftness, the behemoth bolted. That's when I realized the beast hadn't been feeding alone. Thundering hooves erupted all around, sending tremors through the ground. I tensed, waiting for one to make a wrong turn and eviscerate my tent. None did. My little Walrus tent, sagging sides and all, braved the charge. The deafening herd rumbled away into the distance. And then, silence. With trembling fingers I pinched myself. No, this wasn't a dream. It was just another morning in Yellowstone. It was, I realized years later, precisely why I'd come.

My hunch is that this was the same reason Osborne Russell visited Yellowstone in 1834. Russell, a native northeasterner like myself, had also chosen the Lamar Valley. The valley captivated him, nearly prompting him to settle permanently. In his journal he wrote:

> *We stopped at this place and for my own part I almost wished I could spend the remainder of my days in a place like this where happiness and contentment seemed to reign in wild romantic splendor surrounded by majestic battlements which seemed to support the heavens and shut out all hostile intruders.*

In the blink of a bison's eye, I, too, felt the wild romantic splendor Russell wrote about. But now I needed to eat. I wrenched my arms free, wiggled out of my tent, and made a bowl of oatmeal. Still unnerved, my eyes scanned the hillsides as I cradled the bowl in my hands. Here I was, survivor of a solo Yellowstone night and a bison stampede. Why tempt fate any further? Time to find some boardwalks, visitor centers, and more domesticated environs. I licked the innards of my blue enamel bowl, jammed it into my pack with everything else, and began my return trip. With my pack on my back, I bent down and picked up a snapped-off side of an elk antler. Primitive defense. Cumbersome yet also calming.

A few hours later, I emerged upon the large meadow I'd set out in the previous day. My truck was a little gray dot just visible in the roadside pull-off. Unlike yesterday, the pull-off was now clogged with other cars. A line of park visitors stood shoulder to shoulder along the road edge. They seemed to be looking my way. I stopped and studied them through my binoculars. Sure enough, all their attention was focused on me. A wave of self-consciousness washed over me, prompting me to drop the elk antler. Had carrying it violated a park policy? Was I not permitted here? I forced my feet forward. Then a funny thing happened. Instead of lowering their binoculars when I got close, they kept them raised, ignoring me altogether. When I finally got within earshot, my curiosity exploded.

"What were you folks looking at?"

"You mean, you didn't see it?" a woman asked incredulously.

"See what?"

"A wolf was following you!" a man said, looking up from his spotting scope. "It trailed you at a distance for quite some ways. But I've lost it now." Several folks nodded affirmatively. He looked down through his scope again.

Goosebumps shot down my spine. I turned and looked out across the meadow, disbelieving the testimony. I'd been followed?

By a wolf? Lost in thought and focused on the people on the road, I hadn't ever thought to look behind me. How embarrassing! But fantastic, too. I had been stalked at length by a wolf! In Yellowstone! And here I stood, unscathed yet again. "I love not Man the less . . ." Lord Byron wrote, ". . . but Nature more." Right now I too loved Nature more. Wild romantic splendor indeed!

* * *

Osborne Russell was followed in Yellowstone, too. Not by wolves but by a war party of Blackfoot Indians who had a long history in the region. Many tribes had a long history here; Native American presence in Yellowstone began over eleven thousand years ago. Native people including the Crow, Shoshone, and Nez Perce used the varied resources in the park. They hunted animals, chipped out obsidian arrowheads, and my personal favorite, used the many hot springs for cooking and preparing hides. Not long after captains Lewis and Clark passed north of Yellowstone in 1806, fur trappers and adventurers began exploring and exploiting the area. Native communities suddenly found themselves in competition for game. With a history of raiding Crow and Shoshone hunting parties, the Blackfoot, feeling threatened, defended their traditional grounds from the trappers as well. This included Russell, who also was a trapper.

The Blackfoot men caught up with Russell and a friend while they camped. They attacked, skewering Russell with arrows in his hip and leg. Despite crippling wounds, Russell and his friend crawled to the woods and hid out until the Blackfeet disappeared. Justifiably, Russell's friend despaired. Russell, however, was made of something different. In his journal, he later wrote:

He [my friend] exclaimed Oh dear we shall die here, we shall never get out of these mountains, Well said I if you persist [sic] in thinking so you will die but I can crawl from this place upon my hands and one knee and Kill 2 or 3 Elk and make a shelter of the skins dry the meat until we get able to travel.

Russell did just that. He survived his wounds, willed himself to find food and shelter, and left Yellowstone to return back east to his roots. Where I was a poser, Russell was legit. His first date with Yellowstone had been an unmitigated disaster. Even in the midst of his ordeal, Russell fell for the place. He wrote at length about his experiences, unable to escape the intoxication he'd felt.

I also returned east to my roots after my brief visit. And like Russell, Yellowstone went with me. For the next fifteen years, I fluttered around. Grad school in ecology, a long stint in East Africa, a professorship. I became hooked on experiential education over other modes of learning and punctuated the courses I taught with extended trips. With little effort, my students connected concepts to places. If I chose my locations well, many fell head over heels for new landscapes. I taught, yes. But I also aimed, as John Muir wrote, "to entice people to look at Nature's loveliness." All I had to do was get my students out there. Nature did the rest. The Amazon, Africa, Costa Rica, Grand Canyon, Acadia . . . but one place was missing.

Yellowstone.

Multiple times I considered it. I dragged my feet, leery of spoiling the romantic nostalgia that had grown with the years. I was reluctant for another, more important reason, too. The more I unearthed about Yellowstone the more it became clear: it was being loved to death. It was crowded. It was developed. Partly as an outgrowth of this, it was endlessly embroiled in controversy. As Paul Schullery explains in his book *Searching for Yellowstone*, the park had moved from a "bear problem" to an "elk problem" to a "people problem."

I had to agree. I called campgrounds only to discover that they had been booked for months. The campgrounds themselves had become mini-cities, comprising hundreds of sites. The top predator was no longer the grizzly; it was the massive RV. Decades after my memorable first date, I doubted if another rendezvous was worth it. Edward Abbey's deep fears of industrial tourism had surely been borne out. I worried growing as cantankerous as he did, and that I'd come to the same succinct conclusion Rudyard Kipling had during a visit to Yellowstone: "I hate it here."

Last year I finally broke. I decided to pay my estranged lover a visit. The irony was palpable. I would become part of the very problem I feared, adding two vanloads of idealistic students to our nation's first—and most iconic—national park. Back in 1872, Yellowstone had been explicitly created "for the beauty and enjoyment of the people." This return trip of mine would conclude once and for all if any kind of beauty and enjoyment still could be had. Twenty years after my first rapturous visit, could Yellowstone seduce me again?

This time, however, things were different. I had a gaggle of ornithology students. If such a thing is possible, we would steer clear of the tourist game. We weren't after geysers or grandeur; we were after birds. Selfies? No way.

Naturally, I opted to spend at least a day in the Lamar Valley, that magical maze of meadows where I'd stared point blank into a bison's eye and been stalked by a sneaky wolf. Unfortunately, our limited time wouldn't allow a backcountry excursion like I'd had. The valley had only one afternoon to cast its spell.

Growling stomachs dictated the place we chose to park, a random pullout along the northeast entrance road. I wasn't worried; there was no bad place to park along this stretch. The scene before us was an Albert Bierstadt painting: a Lilliputian creek meandering through an endless expanse of green freckled with wandering bison. I divvied up bag lunches as my students sat amidst clumps of aromatic sagebrush. Caught up in memories, I wandered alone down the hill slope. A little brown bird interrupted my jaunt. It popped up from the sage, eyeing me suspiciously. Both of us cocked our heads trying to ID each other. Got it. Its subtle combination of stripes and the habitat it had chosen tipped me off. Brewer's sparrow. "Hey everybody," I called to my students, "here's one of our target birds we need to see!"

My enthusiasm, however, was not returned. This was lunchtime, not class time. Hunger trumped this little brown bird. Worried it might fly off before my students had the chance to see it, I pulled out my camera. The sparrow had no interest in a photo shoot. It took off for a nearby bush. I, however, had no interest in losing the bird. I followed, determined. When I got close, the sparrow again deserted his bush in lieu of another. Again I followed. In the midst of this cat-and-mouse, one of my students cried out from above: "Wolf!"

Goosebumps shot down my spine. I leapt up from my knees. Twenty years after being trailed by a wolf in this very valley, could it really be happening again? I combed the vegetation. Sure enough, a pair of pointed ears approached me. That's all I could see. Sagebrush obscured the rest. Just like before, a line of people formed along the roadside, about twenty-five yards upslope. This time, they were my students. Another gregarious tourist had joined them. It was his voice that rang out.

"If that's your professor down there, he'd better get moving! The wolf is heading his way!"

Despite his alarm, I knew the tourist's histrionics were unfounded. Wolf attacks were exceedingly rare in the United States and when they did happen, were usually related to situations of scarce prey. At a balmy seventy degrees in a prey-rich valley, I doubted I was the target. Three things bothered me nonetheless. One, nature doesn't always follow rules. Two, whatever this animal was, it was coming my way. And three, the ears had disappeared.

"Where is it?!" I yelled up to my line of onlookers, trying to conceal my growing uncertainty.

"Coming straight for you!" the tourist hollered back. He seemed excited by the prospect of this face-off.

Crouching, I quickly pulled out the largest camera lens I had from my bag. If this creature jumped me, my camera would be my billy club. I could also document my demise.

The ears reappeared. Ever so slightly, the animal's head came up and two liquid amber eyes of wild intensity met my own. "An animal's eyes have the power to speak a great language," Martin Buber wrote. I now understood his sentiment. Something in these eyes suggested I was safe. At that point, escape was impossible, even if I'd wanted to. Oddly, I didn't want to; I wanted to extend the moment as long as possible, to see life as this great predator did. My fear had dissipated in the decade and a half since my first Yellowstone adventure. In its place was spellbound curiosity.

With head down, the animal stepped deliberately out from the sagebrush and approached. Eight yards. Five . . . wait a minute! This was no wolf. Way too small and dainty. Clearly a coyote. I shot off some photos and stood up, relieved. Even though just a coyote, it was disconcertingly close. Three yards off, I realized the coyote had little interest in me. I was just another clump of sagebrush. The coyote's gaze went past me, a few feet to my right. It cocked its head slightly and tensed. Suddenly it sprang headlong into a shrub. When it emerged, an unlucky vole squiggled in its jaws.

The coyote caught several more voles before wandering off, to the aggravation of a pair of pronghorn parents. I rejoined my class up along the roadside. Like me, they were giddy. We had blithely wandered into the apotheosis of a nature documentary. The tourist who had delivered the play-by-play high fived us, adamantly insisting it had been a wolf. After a few minutes of friendly debate, he drove off to ferret out another Yellowstone drama he could narrate, embellish, and misconstrue. In the midst of our roadside merriment, one thing stood out. We had been in the right place at the right time. Lucky? For sure. But had we not embarked on our atypical quest, there wouldn't have been any luck to receive. And our goal was clearly atypical. Unlike ninety-nine percent of Yellowstone's other visitors, we were questing after a little brown bird.

The little brown bird—the Brewer's sparrow—was one of a dozen "target birds" I'd tasked my students with finding. The goal was two-fold. First, it drew attention to the underappreciated parts of the park. Second, it transformed our time into a treasure hunt on the grandest scale, a 2.2-million-square-mile ecosystem. We were searching out the needles in the haystack, bland little birds overshadowed on a superlative stage featuring world famous geysers, big shaggy bison, and of course, *Ursus arctos horribilis*, the infamous grizzly bear.

A lovely thing happened to us in the process. Yes, we enjoyed the larger things. But gradually, the larger things gave way to the smaller. The longer our stay, the more bears and bison became background. MacGillivray's warbler stole the show at Tower Falls. Clark's nutcracker headlined Lower Falls. Other key attractions were savored more for the overlooked avifauna they harbored—mountain bluebirds, violet-green swallows, Barrow's goldeneyes—than anything else. Like the coyote's gaze in the Lamar Valley, we were chasing the tiniest. And while the coyote was rewarded in voles, we were rewarded in birds for all their beauty and intricate life histories. It was a coup, subtle but relentless. Yellowstone's mammalian tyranny was overthrown by a democracy of wings.

* * *

The birds gave us something else, too: a way out of Joseph Sax's dilemma concerning the direction of our national parks. In his milestone book, *Mountains Without Handrails*, Sax discusses myriad issues that plague our parks. How much to develop them, whether wildlife should be controlled, if visitors should be regulated . . . the list is long. Of these, Sax wrote most passionately about one: the experience that each visitor has. Specifically, he bemoaned the standardization of prepackaged park experiences. Regarding the Grand Canyon, for example, he wrote:

> *The drearily routine mule rides at the South Rim of the Grand Canyon for which people line up morning after morning; the one-hour, two-hour, four-hour horseback loops, with a daily breakfast ride or 'chuck wagon dinner' thrown in, that are so common a sight; the round-the-lake commercial boat ride that is a standard feature at a number of parks. All these are nothing but amusements, however beautiful the setting, and they seem indistinguishable from the local pony ride. Their capacity to get visitors deep into the park experience seems minimal, they have a mass production quality about them, and they have considerable capacity to detract attention from the fashioning of a personal agenda. They can be dispensed with.*

Sax clearly loved hyperbole. But if you look past the drearily routine mule rides, it's easy to climb aboard the chuck wagon of his thesis. Namely, that deeper experience—meaningful contact with our national parks—has to be cultivated in personal, sometimes offbeat ways. Flouting convention requires creativity. A simple backcountry hike is immune to, in the lingo of Sax, the "banality and predictability" of standard park experiences. The same is true for a kayaking trip, a fly-fishing jaunt, and of course, a week of searching out a list of special little birds. Such activities require self-initiative. As a result, they avoid the mind-numbing contrivance Sax warned about.

Even for those unable or unwilling for such forays off the beaten path, hope isn't lost.

Because hope, I discovered on our last day in the park, is found in the most unlikely of places. Behind a row of maintenance buildings in Mammoth Hot Springs, to be precise. I was scanning the slopes for a sagebrush sparrow, another target bird we hadn't yet found. Unused to seeing a tourist in such an odd spot, a ranger popped out of a back door.

"Whatcha lookin' for?" the uniformed woman asked, adjusting her full-brim hat.

"A sagebrush sparrow," I replied sheepishly, bracing myself for likely confusion. I needn't have. She smiled warmly. It was a smile of complete understanding; one that assured me I'd stumbled into a similar species, who, like the shorebird man of Montrose Point, also appreciated the smaller, overlooked parts of life.

"I think you'll have to head a ways toward Gardiner to find those. Are you staying in Mammoth tonight?"

"Nope, heading south to Headwaters."

"Then you need to see the harlequins!" she exclaimed, pointing at me with both hands. I'll have to give you pretty explicit directions because it's a place where nobody goes."

"I'm all ears," I said.

Two hours later, my students were standing aside the Yellowstone River at a seldom-used pullout. Ten yards out on a gravel bar, glistening in the late afternoon light, were eleven harlequin ducks. The flock was a palette of subtle tones, the males a yin-yang of contrasting colors set off by rich chestnut flanks. Here was perhaps the most sought after of our target birds, ducks that have chosen swift-moving streams as their oyster. Indeed a species to savor, seen by few. The crowds were well behind us. Nor would they ever come. Selfies were snapped with Old Faithful in the background, not a raft of ducks. No, the crowds were still on Sax's standard circuit, shoulder-to-shoulder on boardwalks and bumper-to-bumper at bear jams.

I was glad to enjoy the spectacle away from the crowds. But I was sad, too. I wished people knew how dazzling these ducks looked in their eveningwear. And how the sun lit up the riffles like glittery jewels. I wished they realized greater glories were free to all with minimal effort. The benevolent ranger in Mammoth recognized the deeper connection I—and now my class—had grown to crave. Simple directions had brought us here, a place to celebrate the lesser known and little publicized. Like a night in the Lamar Valley or a lunch on a hillside of sagebrush, all it required was an adventurous spirit and a pinch of initiative.

I should never have doubted my first date with Yellowstone. Yes, the park changed in the twenty or so years since my first visit. It always would. But I had changed too. Our loving compatibility rested on me accepting that.

My students were uncharacteristically quiet. All of us had found a place where, as Osborne Russell wrote over a century earlier, "happiness and contentment seemed to reign in wild romantic splendor."

One of the harlequins suddenly stopped preening. It looked around, stretched each leg methodically, and ambled away from the oblivious flock. With nary a backward glance, it plunged headlong into the cold, bubbling current. Rather than float effortlessly away with the flow, this one focused its gaze upriver. And with all the determination a duck can conjure, it swam away upstream. Paddling perhaps for something even greater.

29 · MORAL OF THE MOURNING DOVES

O Lord of love and kindness, who created the beautiful earth and all the creatures walking and flying in it, so that they may proclaim your glory. I thank you to my dying day that you have placed me amongst them.

—Saint Francis of Assisi

I woke up this morning in a tent that felt like it was flying through a raucous flock of birds. Utter cacophony. I glanced at my sleeping family, nestled supine beside me like sardines. How could they sleep through this? I squinted through blurry eyes at my watch. Five a.m. My stomach gurgled and whined, chastising my overindulgence around the campfire. To celebrate Memorial Day weekend, we had roasted hot dogs and made s'mores. In the midst of the lively conversation I'd lost track of how many hot dogs I'd eaten. Now I was paying the price.

Six hours earlier, as I had crawled into the tent clutching my overburdened stomach, not a peep or warble had pierced the quiescent night. The birds were OFF. But as dawn does every morning, it flipped the switch. ON. Almost instantly, every bird that survived the night insisted on proclaiming three simple facts: I'm alive! No trespassing! Let me sire your kids! Each bird seemed to be shouting into a loudspeaker. No need to go birding today, I thought. I can easily do it from here. I sorted and sifted, filtering out the common species and moving on to the less familiar. American robin, northern cardinal, great-crested flycatcher, mourning warbler, WHAT?! Wait. This one didn't fit. Oh wait, yes, yes. Northern waterthrush. I listened again. Or was it? The beginning notes sounded like a northern. But the rhythm was more like a Louisiana waterthrush.

I lay still as the bird bewitched me. With each rendition, I grew less and less confident. I eased my head off the lump of clothes serving as my pillow. This satisfying game was souring, as if I'd just forgotten the name of an old friend. To restore inner peace, I'd have to lay eyes on this bedeviling songster. But I needed to maintain bodily and familial peace, too. To get up now, I'd risk aggravating my aching intestines, waking up the troops, and dealing with cranky kids all day. And if I forfeited the next hour of sleep chasing this bird, I'd be cranky too. I weighed my choices. Staying in bed was low risk . . . surely the right thing. Climbing over bodies and slipping out undetected would be tougher. The mystery bird sang again. Ever so gingerly, I shimmied out of my cocoon and crawled to the tent door.

Ziiiiip. I unzipped the tent door. This, I quickly realized, cannot be done quietly.

"Where are you going?" Linda could sleep through the kids yelling, knocks at the door, even a ringing bedside phone. But not once, in many years of marriage, had I successfully slipped past her in the dark. Why I thought I could do so in an obnoxiously loud tent was anybody's guess.

"Just to watch the morning," I whispered. Explaining that my real motivation was to decipher the few final notes from the syrinx of a little brown bird would risk waking the kids. And it sounded silly.

"Don't be gone long." Linda spun over in her sleeping bag

with the speed of a croc tearing a slab of meat from a carcass.

"I won't," I replied, clumsily snagging my toes on the half-inch of tent flap on the floor. Losing my balance, I half-somersaulted into the damp grass just outside the door. Someday, I promised myself, I would design a tent solely for birder parents, with noiseless materials for easy, early morning escapes. I regained my footing, peered upward, and quickly located the perpetrator. He was perched on the topmost twig of an old sycamore about thirty yards away, striking a perfect silhouette. With overcast sky behind him, I couldn't discern any subtle plumage variations. The bird threw its head back, singing over and over. If any creature on earth embodies the concept of carpe diem, it's a neotropical warbler in spring.

I focused my binoculars. Okay, definitely a waterthrush. Phew. I wasn't losing my mind entirely. But I needed field marks. I scrambled up a slope, hoping to get eye-level with the bird. If I could find an angle that put vegetation behind him, field marks should appear. It worked. The waterthrush sported a whitish belly without any buff washing on the flanks. Coupled with the song, I was nearly certain this was a northern. A long narrow superciliary stripe would remove any lingering doubt. I needed to see it. At this distance, the only way to get it was to snap a photo, zoom in, and later adjust the image contrast on my computer. That should work. I pulled out my camera with its bazooka-sized lens. The waterthrush with an asterisk stopped singing. It glanced around nervously and crouched down.

I suddenly needed to do the same. In the midst of pulling off the lens cap, my gluttonous night of hot dog consumption had caught up with me. My bowels demanded attention. I dropped my camera in the leaves and wedged my way into a dense thicket. Northern versus Louisiana seemed insignificant to the matters at hand. In the midst of my maneuvering,

I lost focus on the bird. But in that shadowy copse, relieved and staring intently at the leaf litter, another man from another era slowly came into focus. For reasons still unknown, my thoughts turned to Gilbert White.

White was an attentive and first-rate naturalist from the 1700s best known for writing *The Natural History of Selborne*, one of the most treasured books in English literature. He had an eidetic mind, observant and meticulous. Somewhat unfortunately, he is also well known for his steadfast belief that swallows—those avian acrobats that surround us rural country dwellers in the summer months—hibernate. This wouldn't be so bad, writer David Quammen points out, if White had stopped there. Some birds, like the common poorwill of the American Southwest, enter torpor, a quasi-hibernation where the heart slows and body temperature drops. But White ventured further. Not only do swallows hibernate, he hypothesized, they likely hibernate underwater.

Like many others reading White's account for the first time, I snickered at his primitive thoughts. One need not be a first-rate physiologist to realize the impossibility of a pocket-sized, soaking wet bird surviving subzero temperatures. Frogs may be able to do it, but not warm-blooded birds. Regardless of how long ago he lived, Gil should've known better. Didn't he ever step outside after a bath on a cold January morning?

Reflection, however, has curbed my criticism. Granted, White's hypothesis still sounds preposterous. But the fact that he made one is fantastic. I'm neither a first-rate physiologist nor a first-rate naturalist. I jot lots of stuff down in notebooks. But I rarely go farther than that. Unlike Gil, I'm gun shy. White rose to the top of his field by immersing himself in his craft. He embodied Annie Dillard's sentiment in *Pilgrim at Tinker Creek*: "We are here to abet creation and to witness it," she wrote, "to notice each thing so that each thing gets noticed." In Dillard's view, it's grievous indeed to let nature play its great dramas to an empty house. White agreed; he got out there. In an age without handy reference guides, White turned himself into one. He took it one step further, too. Not only did he witness creation, he also witnessed to others about his hypotheses. And hypotheses, even bad ones, are how knowledge—indigenous and scientific—advances.

My backyard, I've come to realize, is also a theater. Night and day, the show plays on without intermission. Out my door is a guaranteed front row seat. All the show requires of me is that I observe it. My observations, regardless how paltry, are the bedrock upon which the scientific method stands. All the great ones—Aristotle, da Vinci, Mendel—relied on them. Where would biology be today without the firsthand insightful scribbles of Darwin and Wallace? Despite their obvious historical importance, direct observation seems to have lost its vogue in today's technologically driven world. While observations used to drive science, they now seem to be riding shotgun. So reliant are we on secondhand information, sometimes they're even stuffed in the trunk.

Why? Surely there are several reasons. One reason, however, could explain most of it. Like Gil, I forged a hypothesis. Observations require being out there. They require initiative. Like lots of things, it's simply easier not to make them than to make them. We are ankle deep in an information-saturated world. It's all too easy to slurp up water from the freely flowing cyber-fountain. In my experience, purer sources require an uphill climb. Secondhand information is perpetually in our pockets, at our bedside at night, literally at our fingertips. A few finger swipes, mouse clicks, audible words . . . *presto!* Information. More than we can ever read or process. Access speed trumps all. But making observations takes time. Herein lies the rub.

Ever slow to adapt, I still prefer a physical book with paper and binding to one that requires periodic plug-ins and power-ups. But even my treasured books, with dog-eared corners and coffee stains, offer me indirect and secondhand info. So regardless of how rapaciously I read, I go no further at my peril. It's fine to stop there. But is it good? Is it the best? I'm reminded of the power of firsthand observation when I recall the first time I stepped into a patch of stinging nettles. They hadn't made an impression in my botanical field guides. With both legs on fire, I learned them instantly. And haven't forgotten.

That's why Gilbert White was great even though his conjecture wasn't. He observed everything. First and foremost he watched. As he did so, he recorded. There wasn't a lazy bone in his body. He made thousands of summertime swallow observations over his lifetime. But try as might, he didn't—and couldn't—observe their wintertime whereabouts. I'm sure he tried. And he likely lamented not knowing where they went when summer turned to fall. Jet planes were still two centuries off. Communication between continents took months, sometimes years. Coordinated bird banding communities didn't exist.

While White may have heard reports of swallows in faraway lands, he had no way of knowing what species they were, or if they were his. When he couldn't observe anything more—when his swallows vanished into thin air as he slept—he was left to speculate. Instead of leaving it there, he looked around, noticed other temperate creatures hibernating, and logically assumed that swallows did so too. When he couldn't do any more, White did the right thing. He sided with William of Ockham. His hypothesis had the fewest assumptions; it was his Ockham's razor. Swallows hibernated, he reasoned. And since he couldn't find them in the soil, they had to be deep in his pond.

* * *

My dismal view of White hung on like a bad cold until one frosty fall evening last November. The white on my mind then was the blanket of snow covering the ground all around me. I was nestled up against a small white pine in an overgrown field. Ostensibly, I was deer hunting. Really, it was another session of therapy, a two-hour time to declutter my mind. The numbness in my toes and the encroaching darkness suggested, however, that my deer-less vigil had drawn to a close. I straightened my stiff legs one at a time and brushed the snow off my lap. Just as I did so, a feathered missile shot past my face. ZOOM! I ducked instinctively. ZOOM! ZOOM! ZOOM! More missiles whizzed past my tree. Then, like heat-seekers, they circled in a tight arc and landed in my tree. A latecomer landed with beguiling grace on a branch not four feet from my face. Statuesque, it scrutinized me. A mourning dove.

I've seen thousands of mourning doves. Probably tens of thousands. This one was different. More likely, I was different. Two hours of stillness had bequeathed a tabula rasa—a psychological blank slate. The early empiricists referred to this as a condition of the mind bereft of ideas imprinted by the senses. While my blank slate wasn't exactly what the empiricists meant by their term, it was markedly less cluttered than normal. My impression of this dove, for the first time in ages, wasn't shaped through secondhand sources. For a timeless moment, I beheld a mourning dove; saw its very doveness. And out of this close encounter flowed patient, firsthand observations.

I was drawn first to the dove's eyes. They were liquid black and lacked a discernible pupil. A thin, powder-blue outline enshrouded each eye. Never once, below my feeders, had I ever noticed this. A small black spot adorned each cheek, about an inch below each eye. They looked like waning crescent moons. I had always thought of mourning doves simply as gray birds. They were more than this. An arm's length away, I noticed lavender, peach, blue, and cream.

Still oblivious to my presence, the dove then confided a secret. One I'd never considered, nor even wondered about: where they spend chilly November nights. Here in this small white pine in an overgrown field, nestled on a stout branch ten inches from the trunk, this dove was settling in. It fluffed out its feathers, turned its head rearward, and buried its fleshy bill into its filigree coverts.

Why hadn't I known this before? Probably because I'd never bothered to go out for a nighttime ramble. For much of my life, I had sat on my laurels, leaning on the stockpile of secondhand info I'd read about nocturnal bird roosting. Until now, that had sufficed. Staring at the mourning dove, the insufficiency of secondhand knowledge suddenly became clear. Knowing birds roost at night didn't seem like knowing much of anything, a ribcage lacking vitals. The substance was in the sub-questions: the where, when, and how.

Gilbert White hadn't relied on secondhand sources. I had been hypocritical deriding his hypotheses. He was a far greater naturalist than myself, yet I'd been too lazy to emulate his far more superior mode of discovery. I know I'll never comprehend many of nature's myriad mysteries. But the mourning dove had a moral: those who let nature play to an empty house, relying only on the observations of others, know even less.

That's why I crawled out of my tent in the wee hours of the morning to look at the waterthrush singing an aberrant song. I had remembered the mourning dove's moral from the previous autumn. In that meaningful encounter, I had awoken from an underwater hibernation of my own. There, watching the waterthrush, firsthand observation reigned supreme. I was learning experientially.

Birds have experiential learning to do, too. And before I

could positively identify my tormentor, it flew off and disappeared, much like White's wintertime swallows. Oddly, I was okay with it. For on a deeper level, I knew I was finally following Gil's lead, building a better foundation upon the bedrock of direct observation. This was indeed the right path of the credible natural historian. And while I'll never know if it was a Louisiana or northern waterthrush, I did conclude one thing with certainty. Memorial Day weekend or not, never again will I lose track of how many hot dogs I eat.

30 · OCD Ecology

*How little I know of that arbor vitae when I have
learned only what science can tell me.*

—Henry David Thoreau

We all do things in our youth we aren't proud of. Moments
when our headstrong zeal takes the wheel of our lives
and delivers us to places unplanned. One of my regrettable moments stands out from the rest. My intentions were fine. But I
was certainly old enough to have known better.

With very little foresight, in the midst of my dissertation
research, I loaded up my dilapidated Land Rover and steered it
toward the roadless stretches south of Serengeti National Park,
in Tanzania. This time I wasn't seeking an indigenous bird. I
was seeking indigenous people.

Rumor and hearsay had brought me this far. In my early
twenties, this was enough. A friend, Dennis, had heard of a few
bands of Hadzabe people—or Hadza—who were hunter-gatherers eking out a living in the arid thorn scrub south of Serengeti. We should try to find them, he casually suggested one day.
That's all I needed. A few weeks later, our Land Rovers were
lurching along the plains in pursuit of Hadza people, spitting
up a dust cloud that hung in the air long after we'd passed.

The plains surrendered to bush and our single-track road
disappeared altogether. We eased our arthritic cars around
trees, boulders, and aardvark holes. Anxiety crept in with every

tree I clipped. A breakdown here would necessitate abandonment of a vehicle, possibly for good. As bad as my car was, I couldn't afford to lose it; my research depended entirely upon mobility.

At the same time I only felt partly culpable. I could pin any fate that befell me on the dozens of old anthropological adventure books I'd long marinated in. In The Forest People, for example, anthropologist Colin Turnbull gleaned incredible insights from the lives of the Pygmies in Congo's Ituri forest. With little more than a pith helmet and a clipboard, Turnbull courageously immersed himself in a culture long cut off from civilization. I now wanted to do the same. Run from what cantankerous writer Ed Abbey called "syphilization" and study something authentic and indigenous. Good intentions indeed. My regret, of course, is never once thinking what my bombastic and unexpected arrival would mean to the Hadza communities.

Buoyed along on such misguided romantic visions, and several dead ends later, we finally rolled into a Hadza "settlement." A half dozen nearly invisible grass huts sat under the colossal arms of baobab trees. Justifiably surprised by the sudden appearance of two growling Land Rovers, many men and women immediately melted into the surrounding bush. Dennis and I climbed out, determined to allay fears and spend the afternoon learning what we could from some of the world's last remaining hunter-gatherers.

Our smiles and Swahili slowly spread the message that we posed little threat. One by one, Hadza men and women, some barely reaching my chest, reemerged from the bush. I cracked nuts with children, shook hands with old leathery women, and crawled in and out of houses on all fours. As if prepping for an exam, I ceaselessly asked questions and crammed in as many plant and animal names as I could. Most dumbfounding of all, of course, was each family's utter lack of belongings. A few animal skins, bows, a slingshot, and some homemade knives; the whole band's goods would maybe fill a wheelbarrow. Here were people who lived lightly upon the earth. I jotted down notes, took a few pictures, and then, very reluctantly, rumbled away with Dennis.

The question I now ask myself is why. Beyond the obvious rudeness of my intrusion, why did indigenous peoples enchant me so much? What was I so urgently seeking in my early twenties? Now in my fourth decade of life, I've edged a bit closer to an answer. All because of a helpful clue I stumbled upon from an unlikely source: a short essay about Henry David Thoreau.

It's hard to love natural history without also loving Thoreau. Anybody who writes lyrical prose about the healing salve of nature is a definite friend of mine. Unlike many devotees, however, my love has waxed and waned the deeper I've delved. It waned when I discovered Thoreau wasn't nearly the rugged hermit he portrayed himself to be in the pages of *Walden*. But it has waxed, almost blindingly so, after I stumbled upon an essay entitled, "Walden's Man of Science," by Walter Harding.

Like other critics, Harding points out the many natural history blunders Thoreau made in his journals. Thoreau, for example, repeatedly confused the black-throated blue warbler with the indigo bunting. This is head scratching indeed. To the birders in my circle, this is like mistaking a baseball for a Frisbee.

Nor, for that matter, could Thoreau ever ascertain the presence of the ubiquitous ovenbird, a bird I've spent hours observing at close range. Seriously? Did Henry walk blindfolded through the forests around Walden Pond?

Thoreau drew all sorts of wrongheaded conclusions about woodpeckers, thrushes, and prairie chickens, and, for the life of him, couldn't discern red-breasted from white-breasted nuthatches. Such mistakes merit critique. But I prefer applause. Go

Thoreau! A sometimes bumbling, mistake-prone naturalist is a kindred spirit indeed. Here was a guy who plied his craft well before field guides, audio recordings, and eBird. Like Gilbert White in Europe, Thoreau watched, recorded, conjectured, and had the patience—and guts—to write it all down.

Sure he made mistakes. He got a lot right, too. Subsequent studies have shown that Thoreau's theories about forest succession, seed dispersal, and thermal stratification in water bodies were spot on. And in the midst of his theorizing, his ever-observant eye discovered previously unrecorded species of fish, reptile, and mammal. Through his endless speculations on everything from clouds to glowworms, he became, as Harding points out, the first bona fide American ecologist.

He was also the first ecologist with what had to be OCD. He had maniacal devotion to his journals. For over twenty-five years, Thoreau laboriously recorded all he saw, and heard, and felt, and touched, and tasted. In over two million words! His prescient observations spanned the gamut—ornithology, meteorology, phenology, geology, and limnology, some "ologies" before they were even fields of study. In one of his final journal observations, Thoreau noted faint ridges of sand behind pebbles in a railroad bed to discern the direction rain had arrived. Faint ridges of sand behind pebbles! Had he been born a Hadza, I'm convinced he'd have out-hunted and out-gathered everybody.

But Thoreau wasn't born a Hadza. He was born in 1817, the son of a humble pencil maker. He was the grandson of immigrants, as non-indigenous to America as they come. As a result, the myriad journal observations and measurements he made advanced science, western science. This is why, as Harding points out, Thoreau was "Walden's man of science."

Over his lifetime, Thoreau made 8,433 ornithological entries. The great Harvard ornithologist Ludlow Griscom seized upon these meticulous entries to publish *Birds of Concord*, an incredible ornithological accomplishment that became the first study of bird population dynamics over the course of an entire century. Other keen botanists and meteorologists utilized Thoreau's journals in similar fashion. Even after his death, science owed a debt to observant, obsessive Thoreau.

Like Thoreau, I was born into a non-indigenous world dominated by the scientific method and western ways of knowing. I'm not complaining. The advancements made through western science are profound indeed. I'm grateful for every vaccine and technological leap it has produced. But I'm also leery. And with every year I age, my leeriness increases. Why? For the simple fact that western science is not indigenous. And indigenous knowledge, I'm convinced, is as valuable and endangered as the Hadza themselves.

This is the crux: if indigenous knowledge disappears, so too does a view of nature. One that embodies a wealth of wisdom and experience gained over millennia, culturally embedded and passed down orally over many generations. It is a cumulative body of knowledge and most importantly, it emphasizes relationships that living beings have with one another. While exceptions always occur, many indigenous peoples are more interested in preserving their own social, cultural, and environmental stability than they are in maximizing production. Nature is not, to people like the Hadza, a mere collection of commodities.

Robert Frost was right. Two roads diverged in a yellow wood. Instead of taking the road less traveled by, we products of the Enlightenment are stampeding down the trampled path. With a growing economy always the goal, fellow travelers on this path view nature as little more than a storehouse of goods. Maximum sustainable yields and externalized costs supplant stability, integrity, and sustainability along this rapacious route.

Western science and indigenous knowledge are indeed

different paths of knowledge. But as scholar Fulvio Mazzocchi has pointed out, they are rooted in the same reality. Both ways of knowing have much to offer. We emphasize one over the other only at our peril.

Yes, we all do things we aren't proud of. Sometimes, thank heavens, we are granted opportunities for modest redemption. Me? I've shamelessly copied Thoreau. No, I haven't moved a few miles out of town, written a timeless transcendental classic, nor snuck home for cookies on the weekends (yes, Thoreau often did). I've done something far simpler. Journals. Small enough to slide into a pocket, climb up a ravine, and not realize it's there. My entries are whimsical and sporadic. On September 27, 2016, for example, I recorded the following:

Odd behavior. Behind Fancher, a hairy woodpecker entered a WB nuthatch hole and pulled out either feathers or nest lining. The nuthatch loitered around calling incessantly. Was it preparing a roosting hole for winter? ~2pm. Sunny.

A five-second sketch accompanies the entry. That's it. Similar simple entries follow it page after page. Under-wing patterns of overflying hawks, fox track measurements, first of year warbler appearances. Lots of thought fragments. Occasional numbers and statistics. I'm now on my sixth journal. Each one, over time, becomes part of me, like a limb. They become sacred. I suffered three panic-stricken minutes in Lassen Volcanic National Park last year because I thought I'd lost a journal. The world fortunately came back into focus when I found it wedged into the crease of the passenger seat in my car. Maybe bigger is better after all.

I have no visions of grandeur. No incredible scientific advances are going to spawn one day from my hapless observations. Nor do I need to be buried with them when I die. These journals are for right now. The moments I'm tromping around in the woods and switched on. A journal in my pocket sharpens my eye, focuses my concentration, and deepens my interactions. Each one is rough, worn, and dirty. That doesn't matter. They're not a product. They're process. And sometimes, when I find myself in a mind-numbing academic meeting, I slyly pull one out and page through my thoughts. They awaken me anew. Almost at once, I feel the breeze on my face and the forest underfoot.

More importantly, journal-keeping allows me, a born and bred product of western ways of knowing, to cultivate something that feels more indigenous. No, it's not an accumulation of knowledge passed down over millennia. But it is autochthonous; knowledge accrued by a place's inhabitant. It's local, it's tacit, and it feels more rooted. It allays my fears somewhat and buoys my hope in fostering a more holistic way of viewing the world. I like to think I'm practicing indigenous science, a hybrid knowledge I can pass along to others along my path. My journals are merely a tool of conveyance.

A few months ago, after an afternoon of ice-skating with my kids at a friend's birthday party, I was driving a carload home when I noticed something odd hanging from a telephone wire. Unable to help myself, I pulled over.

"Ezra, look!"

"What?"

"Is that a skunk carcass draped over the power line?"

"Uh, I think so."

"Weird."

"What do you think did that?!"

"A raptor?"

"Maybe. I was thinking an owl . . ."

For a few minutes, the backseat pontificated about a possible perpetrator. Then, like most conversations, it soon switched to the more relevant topics of a kid's life: fairies and Pokémon.

I let it go for a time. Sure enough, as soon as I got home, I pulled out the journal from a pants pocket and made a quick sketch of the carcass. Why? Because it was odd. The skunk didn't drape itself over the power line. Something was responsible. Maybe someday, I'd notice something else in nature, jot it down, and connect the dots. Even if I didn't, I'd go to bed speculating. My imagination had a full tank.

I think I did it for another reason too. Simply because Thoreau would have. And while the Hadza people wouldn't have penned it in a journal, they certainly would have written it in their minds. They'd have noticed it, remembered it, and made multiple connections.

To some, it's just another sketch in just another journal. For me, it is yet another step along my one-man quest for indigenous science. A simple step to help ensure I'll forever remain on the road less traveled. Compared to blasting into the lives of the Hadza people, this is a far better way to seek indigenous ways of knowing. Like Henry, I'll play with the cards I'm dealt. Because when it comes to observing nature, one can never be too Thoreau.

31 · NEVER AGAIN...
UNTIL NEXT TIME

I am a sworn enemy of convention. I despise the conventional in anything.

—Hedy Lamarr

I looked at my watch. I looked at my computer screen. And back at my watch. The digits went blurry as I weighed my impending decision. Could I make it there and back by dinnertime? Did I really need to prepare class for tomorrow? Could I skip that committee meeting? Could I cancel that appointment with the student? Would the bird even be there?

The last question hung in front of me like a slowly dying party balloon. For birders on tight schedules with endless work and familial obligations, the question forms the heavy, dark cloud that obscures what would otherwise be a joyful, carefree quest. The math is simple: Responsibilities are endless. Time is finite. If I sacrifice half a day for birding now, I'll need to make it up later. In my case, it'll result in a late night when sane people are sleeping. Ultimately, it'll lead me to more coffee, bloodshot eyes, a compromised immune system, and probably some shoddy work. This is the cold, hard calculus of birding. Time and tasks are rational, but we birders are not.

Even if you deftly rearrange your schedule and get the math right, there's a deeper problem: birds fly. This physiological phenomenon causes the great angst—and the deep thrill—of birding. Birds are superheroes. Although they forego tights and capes, they can appear suddenly and unexpectedly. Their fickle itineraries are inscrutable, and they often depart well before we'd like them to.

Ultimately this dynamism is why I bird. I go about my daily routine with a pretense of normalcy. But one eye remains fixed on my feathered neighbors. My country, all three acres of it, is strictly patrolled. Best of luck to any foreign interlopers trying to pass through undetected. This same dynamism may explain why despite having met hundreds of birders, I've yet to meet a "mammaler." A Floridian can wake up in April and find a hungry Cape May warbler flitting about the saw palmetto. But never will drawn blinds reveal a migrant moose draining the birdbath.

As a rule, I ignore most rare bird alerts. I scan them like I do obituaries, dispassionately making note of who's gone and who's still around. But sometimes, a rare bird is simply too rare to ignore. This was one of those: a brown booby hanging around Buffalo. Brown boobies, for the record, have absolutely no business in Buffalo. They are gangly seabirds of the New World tropics, enjoying warmer seas and islands for breeding. Stoically I maintained composure and carried out the basic functions of life. After several long and conflicted days, the directionally impaired seabird appeared on the eleven o'clock news. Temptation proved too strong. I caved.

Normally I linger after dismissing a class. I talk to students about life, erase the blackboard, and meander to my next appointment. Not this day. As soon as I'd uttered the words "See you Wednesday," I shot for the door and hurtled down the science building's staircase. In a rare bird chase, every second counts. With my decision finally made, I was optimistic and adrenalized, feeling like an overgrown puppy let off a leash. I jumped in my car and took off down the highway, giddy with the chase.

Untold miles later, I stole a glance at the clock. The hour-and-a-half trip seemed to be taking forever. Doubts crept up like a skulking wren. This wouldn't do. I reached for the radio knob and cranked up a country song. Even the earsplitting twang couldn't dissipate the black cloud darkening my mood.

Why, Eli why?! I had papers to grade, kids at home, and a lawn to mow. These three hours could not be reclaimed. All for what? One gooney bird. With oversized feet, a dorky expression, and a name that made me blush. This was a fool's errand for a ribald retiree, not an overscheduled, self-conscious young father. I stared straight ahead, willing myself to ignore the dashboard clock. The miles ticked by, my grip on the wheel tightening with every passing billboard.

At last I pulled into the Buffalo harbor, the place where the booby had most recently been reported. The sun was slowly sliding away. As soon as I got out of the car, my hopes slid away, too. I knew I had missed the bird.

There is a rule associated with well-publicized rare birds. Each one comes with a fawning horde of obsessive, nature-loving paparazzi. Before me, however, was an empty waterfront. So empty that tumbleweed and a far-off wolf howl would have been fitting. All at once, a mountain of regret collapsed on top of me. Just like the mountain of ungraded papers and shirked responsibilities would upon my arrival home.

But hope dies hard. Defiantly, I raised my binoculars and scanned every ripple and pier. Back and forth. Back and forth. Other than some sleepy cormorants on a far-off break wall, nothing. Just placid Lake Ontario waters. Before me lay a harbor of tranquility, contrasting sharply with my building inner storm.

A pair of lovestruck teenagers sauntered past, hand in hand.

They saw nothing but each other. I should be hand in hand with Linda right now. Or at the very least, helping her set the table. I scowled. My heart black as a cormorant's plumage, I wanted to shove the giggling lovebirds into the water.

I had sacrificed much. Didn't I deserve this bird? Apparently, happy endings only happened in Hollywood, not Buffalo. My grip loosened on my binoculars, my defiance devolving into defeat. I plodded back to the car like a tired basset hound, unable to enjoy the stunning crimson sunset mirrored magnificently in the glassy water. I tossed my binoculars onto the passenger seat, collapsed into my car, and began a long, gloomy drive home.

Socrates said that the unexamined life is not worth living. Okay then, now was the time to examine mine. Glowering, I switched off the radio. In birder lingo, I'd just "dipped." Dipping isn't uncommon. But like most naïve, overly optimistic people, I assumed it only happened to other people. Yes, if you chase birds, you're occasionally going to dip. To some, this gamble—this rolling of the dice—is the best part of the game. Many chasers I've met handle it with style and grace, morphing their misses into fuel for the next round. Some even learn to laugh about it.

Not me. Not now. I was still too angry for ego-saving legerdemain. I had dipped, plain and simple. I had forsaken responsibility, squandered time, and now had nothing but bitterness to show for it.

My chase, however, was chock-full of contradiction. I knew myself. Had I seen the blasted booby, I'd be smiling and singing full out with the radio, regardless of genre. I'd thoroughly enjoy the self-congratulatory drive, all the while extoling my deft decision-making and lauding my bird-chasing abilities. But the booby had beaten me. The smug seabird hung in my mind's eye, leering at me as it preened its feathers from some godforsaken buoy just out of reach of my binocular-aided vision.

The bird had been on the waterfront for several days. Plenty of people had seen it. Even the local news had managed to find it. So why had it suddenly up and left? Was it hunger? A rambunctious golden retriever? An inadvertent car horn? A clueless kayaker? Or was it something deeper? Like migratory instinct? Maybe it left because, heaven forbid, the gaggle of overzealous birders grew too large? The list of possibilities was endless. The more I thought about it, the more brainless I seemed. Yes, I had devoted hours of a busy day to the abject whimsy of a bicolored seabird.

Nearing home I made a promise. Never again would I chase a bird so wantonly. Sure, bird chasing was a cheaper form of gambling and far more amenable to my all-too-thin wallet. Granted, I loved to roll the dice. But the time sacrifice was too much, ill-conceived for this phase of life. Nature-loving cheapskate or not, never again would I be lured into one of nature's fickle casinos.

For many of our more unfortunate moments in life, a well-honed selective memory is a godsend. Like so many others, my brown booby debacle was soon swept away by the stewards of my ego-saving psyche. I moved on and kept my vow, resuming my conservative ways. All the other rare birds that paid western New York a visit that year flew away unseen. I deleted the rare bird alerts, swore off eBird, and stayed the course. I'll get them in retirement, I consoled myself, marking a B+ atop a student paper I was grading.

A year passed. On a short, work-related trip to southern California, I joyfully discovered that my itinerary allowed a half-day of freedom. A rare window of time in a really birdy place. Too rare and too special to burn up in a coffee shop. I drove down to the Ventura harbor, plunked down some money, and jumped aboard a tour boat that ferries passengers back and forth to the Channel Islands. Time didn't allow for an exploration of the ecologically intriguing islands. But it did allow a few hours of scanning the skies and the seas. Accompanying me were various lighthearted day-trippers and school groups.

My fellow seafarers were avidly seeking whales, sea lions, and a short reprieve from the crowded coast. My expectations were remarkably low. This was a ferryboat, and I was likely the lone birder aboard. Nor had I planned the trip in advance. But birds were everywhere. Despite the choppy waves and the boat's fast, unrelenting speed, I ticked off pink-footed shearwaters, pelagic cormorants, and even a Cassin's auklet. Pure ecstasy.

The bird gods had apparently been appeased that fine day in the channel. More benevolence soon issued forth. As we neared Anacapa Island, the captain cut back the throttle. Student groups ambled over to the railings squealing with delight. Harbor seals lay across the jagged rocks like throw cushions. A pod of dolphins encircled our boat, plunging off the bow like torpedoes. And then, seemingly out of nowhere, seabirds appeared. Hundreds. Maybe thousands. Cormorants, gulls, pelicans . . . and most unbelievably, a booby.

"We've got a real treat today," the captain exclaimed over the crackly PA system. "A blue-footed booby. This is a bird we rarely see on these tours. Tends not to venture this far north."

Standing behind a wall of students, I stared at the gaudy booby, transfixed. The bird appeared as mystified by its goofy blue feet as I was. The booby wasn't alone. As the boat bobbed, I noticed another standing just off to the right. This one was mottled brown and white and lacked the other's powder-blue feet. Must be a juvenile blue-footed, I thought, smiling. Two for the price of one.

My musing ended when the captain again cut in. "This is incredible," he exclaimed. "Not only do we have a blue-footed booby, but there's another even rarer bird on the same rock!" He trailed off for a moment, intentionally building suspense. Here was a captain par excellence. Riding shotgun on his boat was just fine.

By now, I didn't need the captain to finish his sentence. Some days, some moments, are just for us. They're meant to be; the planets align and everything is effortless. I knew exactly who this rare bird was. It was no immature blue-footed. This was my former nemesis, the very bird that had caused me to scowl and stew and blow a half-day in Buffalo. One that had caused me to renew a vow of sanity and pledge to lead a more balanced life.

"Yes, folks, this is a really rare sighting," the captain proclaimed. "A brown booby!" From the lilt in his voice, he was just as excited as I was. "Just what it's doing way up here in the Channel Islands is anybody's guess."

I had a guess, however. Victorious at last, I raised my arms in triumph, my smile irrepressible. A few of my fellow seafarers eyed me suspiciously. I suppressed the urge to run up and grab the captain's microphone. I wanted to tell my fellow passengers why the brown booby was here on Anacapa Island. I lacked an ecological reason. But I sure had a cosmic one.

This bird was here for me. A reminder, an avian Post-it Note, with a simple message. Yes, a well-balanced life is virtuous. But adventurous spontaneity is virtuous, too. My joy was due in part to that blown day in Buffalo. Sure, any bird that turns up in an unexpected place is cool. But the really satisfying part— the deep, visceral stuff I was feeling—was directly linked to all that earlier time spent searching. I may have gone bankrupt in Buffalo, but I cashed in at the Channel Islands.

I like to think I manage my birding well and keep it in the bounds of a balanced life. I show up for work regularly. I try to do the dishes and throw a football with my son. For the most part, I ignore the rare bird alerts. But my vows of sanity have been rescinded a smidge. Every now and then, if a really good bird pops up, I glance down at my watch, finger the car keys in my pocket, and nervously glance at my day planner.

The old cycle returns. Optimism. Doubts. Teetering. Sometimes I stay. Other times, I remember the lesson of Anacapa Island: reward depends on the investment. Yes, serendipity sometimes drops out of the sky. But there's a deeper, more satisfying kind of joy out there, too. It's exceedingly rare and depends upon effort. That kind of joy, you just may need to chase.

About Eli J. Knapp

Eli J. Knapp, Ph.D., is professor of intercultural studies and biology at Houghton College and director of the Houghton in Tanzania program. Knapp is a regular contributor to *Birdwatcher's Digest*, *New York State Conservationist*, and other publications. An avid birdwatcher, hiker, and kayaker, he lives in Fillmore, New York, with his wife and children.

Torrey House Press

Voices for the Land

The economy is a wholly owned subsidiary of the environment, not the other way around.

—Senator Gaylord Nelson, founder of Earth Day

Torrey House Press is an independent nonprofit publisher promoting environmental conservation through literature. We believe that culture is changed through conversation and that lively, contemporary literature is the cutting edge of social change. We strive to identify exceptional writers, nurture their work, and engage the widest possible audience; to publish diverse voices with transformative stories that illuminate important facets of our ever-changing planet; to develop literary resources for the conservation movement, educating and entertaining readers, inspiring action.

Visit www.torreyhouse.org for reading group discussion guides, author interviews, and more.

FORTHCOMING FROM TORREY HOUSE PRESS

Mostly White
by Alison Hart
Beginning in 1890, four generations of mixed-race women fight through inter-generational trauma and move toward the healing brought by nature, music, and triumphant resilience.

The Oasis This Time: Living and Dying with Water in the West
by Rebecca Lawton
Water is seen as murderer, savior, benefactor, and Holy Grail in many arid North American communities. Fifteen essays on natural and faux oases explore human attitudes toward water in the West, from Twentynine Palms, California, to Sitka, Alaska.

Standoff: Standing Rock, the Bundy Movement, and the American Story of Occupation, Sovereignty, and the Fight for Sacred Lands
by Jacqueline Keeler
This comparative analysis of the roots of the 2016 Bundy take-over of Malheur Wildlife Refuge and the Sioux Nation's stand-off at Standing Rock asks if the West has really been won—and for whom.

AVAILABLE NOW FROM TORREY HOUSE PRESS

Edge of Morning: Native Voices Speak for the Bears Ears
edited by Jacqueline Keeler
In support of tribal efforts to protect the Bears Ears area of the Four Corners, Native writers bear testimony to the fragile and essential nature of this sacred landscape in America's remote red rock country. Through poem and essay, these often-ignored voices explore the ways many Native people derive tradition, sustenance, and cultural history from the Bears Ears.

Red Rock Stories: Three Generations of Writers Speak on Behalf of Utah's Public Lands
edited by Stephen Trimble
Red Rock Stories conveys spiritual and cultural values of Utah's canyon country through essays and poems of writers whose births span seven decades. First delivered to decision makers in Washington as a limited-edition chapbook, this art-as-advocacy book explores the fierce beauty of and the dangers to ecological and archaeological integrity in this politically embattled corner of wild America.

River of Lost Souls: The Science, Politics, and Greed Behind the Gold King Mine Disaster
by Jonathan P. Thompson
Thompson digs into the science, politics, and greed behind the 2015 Gold King Mine disaster and unearths a litany of impacts wrought by a century and a half of mining, energy development, and fracking in southwestern Colorado.

Nature, Love, Medicine: Essays on Wildness and Wellness
edited by Thomas Lowe Fleischner
A diverse array of people share personal stories that reveal a common theme: when we pay conscious, careful attention to our wider world, we strengthen our core humanity.

Stony Mesa Sagas
by Chip Ward
In this seriocomic environmental novel, Luna Waxwing and Hip Hop Hopi navigate the cultural conflicts of the new American West while learning to live lightly but joyously on the land.

The Talker
by Mary Sojourner
The unforgettable characters in *The Talker* inhabit the present-day Southwest in the fragile, spare, and harsh beauty of the

desert.

29
by Mary Sojourner
Nell, a washed-out executive, falls into an impossible affair and a battle over sacred Native American lands in Twentynine Palms, California.

Inhabited
by Charlie Quimby
A realtor's boom-and-bust town needs a boost, and there's only one barrier to overcome—the people she's supposed to help.

Monument Road
by Charlie Quimby
Leonard Self knows where he's going to end his life. But the road there is winding, and he has company.

Luckiest Scar on Earth
by Ana Maria Spagna
Charlotte, a fourteen-year-old snowboarder, reunites with her father and triumphs over a harrowing backcountry accident and a contentious environmental lawsuit.

The Story of My Heart
by Richard Jefferies, as rediscovered by Brooke and Terry Tempest Williams
A nineteenth-century love letter to nature is rediscovered by Brooke and Terry Tempest Williams.

Yosemite Fall: A National Park Mystery
by Scott Graham
Archaeologist Chuck Bender arrives with his family in the beautiful Yosemite Valley to study the 150-year-old murders of a pair of gold prospectors—while facing down a ruthless killer on the loose.

Yellowstone Standoff: A National Park Mystery
by Scott Graham
When Yellowstone's wolves and grizzlies inexplicably go rogue, archaeologist Chuck Bender protects his family and the scientists accused of murder.

Mountain Rampage: A National Park Mystery
by Scott Graham
Archaeologist Chuck Bender outwits an unknown killer in Colorado's Rocky Mountain National Park when his brother-in-law is accused of murder.

Canyon Sacrifice: A National Park Mystery
by Scott Graham
Archaeologist Chuck Bender races to save his kidnapped daughter as ancient and modern cultures collide in Grand Canyon National Park.

Cold Blood, Hot Sea
by Charlene D'Avanzo
Oceanographer Mara Tusconi sets out to study Maine's warming waters, but finds murder at sea instead aboard research vessel Intrepid.

Alibi Creek
by Bev Magennis
On a remote ranch in New Mexico, a wayward cowboy becomes the catalyst for change in his devout sister's life.

Howl: Of Woman and Wolf
by Susan Imhoff Bird
Bird's compelling exploration of wolves and the people who care about them reveals profound truths—about herself and about our world.

Hawks Rest: A Season in the Remote Heart of Yellowstone

by **Gary Ferguson**
With a new introduction by revered western writer Gary Ferguson, this updated classic explores the wildness, people, and politics of Yellowstone.

Through the Woods: A Journey Through America's Forests
by **Gary Ferguson**
A conversational journey through America's forests, introducing readers to people whose lives are intertwined with the soul of the woods. With a new introduction by the author.

Pale Harvest
by **Braden Hepner**
In a sublime landscape, Jack Selvedge struggles against betrayal to save his farm, Mormon faith, and the girl he loves.

Microfarming for Profit: From Garden to Glory
by **Dave DeWitt**
A candid, well-planned guide on how to turn unused property into an efficient, fun, and profitable microfarm.

Spirit Walk
by **Jay Treiber**
Haunted by a violent episode from his past, a college professor revisits the rugged border country of his youth.

Wild Rides and Wildflowers: Philosophy and Botany with Bikes
by **Scott Abbott and Sam Rushforth**
Two university professors set out to repeatedly bike the Great Western Trail to observe and write about its variations with every season, but their loves and lives become the real adventure.

Facing the Change: Personal Encounters with Global Warming
edited by **Steven Pavlos Holmes**

With courage and honesty, writers and poets from across the United States—and Malaysia—show how one of the major issues of our time is affecting the everyday lives of people today.

The Ordinary Truth
by Jana Richman
Today's western water wars and one family's secrets divide three generations of women as urban and rural values collide in this contemporary novel.

Recapture
by Erica Olsen
This captivating short story collection explores the canyons, gulches, and vast plains of memory along with the colorful landscapes of the West.

Tributary
by Barbara K. Richardson
A courageous young woman flees polygamy in 1860s Utah but finds herself drawn back to the landscapes that shaped her.

The Legend's Daughter
by David Kranes
These fast-paced stories set in contemporary Idaho explore intricate dynamics between fathers and sons, unlikely friends, people and place.

The Scholar of Moab
by Steven L. Peck
Philosophy meets satire, poetry, cosmology, and absurdity in this tragicomic brew of magical realism and rural Mormon Utah.

A Bushel's Worth: An Ecobiography
by Kayann Short
Rooted where the Rocky Mountains meet the prairie, Short's

love story of land celebrates our connection to soil and each other, and one community's commitment to keeping a farm a farm.

Evolved: Chronicles of a Pleistocene Mind
by Maximilian Werner
With startling insights, Werner explores how our Pleistocene instincts inform our everyday decisions and behaviors in this modern day Walden.

Grind
by Mark Maynard
The gritty realism of Hemingway joins the irreverence of Edward Abbey in these linked short stories set in and around Reno, Nevada.